MW00614645

A Gift For:

_____

From:

_____

Have a Blessed Day

A Year of Daily Devotions *from the* Church Health Center

Butch Odom

Published on the Occasion of the
25th Anniversary of the
Church Health Center

Church Health Center
Memphis, TN

About the Church Health Center

The Church Health Center seeks to reclaim the Church's biblical commitment to care for our bodies and our spirits. The Center's ministries provide health care for the working uninsured and promote healthy bodies and spirits for all. To learn more about the Center, visit www.ChurchHealthCenter.org. To learn more about our magazine on health ministry *Church Health Reader*, visit www.chreader.org.

Have a Blessed Day: A Year of Daily Devotions from the Church Health Center © 2012 Church Health Center, Inc. Memphis, TN.

Scripture quotations contained herein are from the *New Revised Standard Version Bible*, copyright 1989, Division of Christian Education of the National Council of the Churches of Christ in the United States of America, and are used by permission. All rights reserved.

ISBN: 978-1-62144-019-2

Printed in the United States of America.

Written by Butch Odom

Edited by Anna Broadwell-Gulde and Susan Martins Miller

Design by Lizy Heard

Photos courtesy of Rachel Thompson Davis, Lizy Heard, Jeff Hulett, Natalie Martin, Marius Penczner, and Alison Tucker

The Church Health Center welcomes your feedback. Please send your comments to FCO@churchhealthcenter.org.

To Mom and Dad,
Carol and Bill Odom, who taught me
the meaning of faith and justice
and instilled in me
a lifelong love of the church.

This is the day the Lord has made;
let us rejoice and be glad in it.

<small>PSALM</small> 118:24

Foreword

In 1987, we opened the doors of our clinic to serve the working uninsured of Memphis. Butch Odom came to the Church Health Center a few years later and has brought a gentle spirit to our workplace.

I begin each morning by reading a devotion from Butch. He has sent these devotions to each staff member of the Church Health Center for more than five years now. His words often linger with me throughout the day. They remind me of something I need to do, a relationship I need to mend, or a part of my life I haven't tended to enough.

Butch has collected the best of his devotions in this volume, *Have a Blessed Day*. These devotions do just that: they remind us that we are indeed blessed by God. They also call us to care for ourselves and each other, even as we care for people among us who are most in need. These devotions center us and remind us of our mission.

I am happy to share with you this book published in celebration of the Church Health Center's 25th anniversary. In our earliest days, our mission was to reclaim the Church's biblical commitment to care for our bodies and our spirits. We are still doing this work today 25 years later.

May these devotions bless you in your own life and inspire you to care for all bodies and spirits.

—G. Scott Morris
Founder and Executive Director
Church Health Center

Introduction

These devotions began as an Advent gift for my Church Health Center coworkers and grew into what you hold in your hands today. It was my hope that these simple devotions would serve as a daily reminder that our work here is God's work. I also wanted them to be a daily blessing to the people we serve as well as to each other and ourselves. For this reason, I ended each one with *Have a Blessed Day*.

At the Church Health Center, we weave a thread of faith through all we do. We have a great diversity of Christian voices and other faith traditions present here, and I wrote these devotions in a way that honors this diversity. The Center also has a wide array of practitioners from doctors to exercise specialists to nutritionists. I wanted to speak across these lines to what links us together in ministry: our call to care for our bodies and our spirits, and in particular, to care for those in need.

I want to offer my deepest thanks to all the employees of the Church Health Center who gave me advice and encouragement through the years. My wife Debbie and my Mom and Dad have been there for me as I wrote each of these devotions. I could not have done this without their ceaseless support.

It has been a blessing in my life to write these devotions each day. I hope reading them will bless you as much as the writing of them has blessed me.

Have a blessed day.

—Butch Odom

Have a
Blessed Day

Are any among you sick? They should call for the elders of the church and have them pray over them, anointing them with oil in the name of the Lord.

JAMES 5:14

Gracious God, help us be fully present for the people we meet today. May we be a healing presence for each person.

Amen.

January

On the Wellness exercise court.

January 1

Then I saw a new heaven and a new earth; for the first heaven and the first earth had passed away, and the sea was no more. And I saw the holy city, the new Jerusalem, coming down out of heaven from God, prepared as a bride adorned for her husband.

REVELATION 21:1–2

Happy New Year! May we work toward this vision of a new Jerusalem, where "mourning and crying and pain will be no more " (verse 4).

Gracious, loving God, be with us in all we do. May we serve one another in ways that build your kingdom toward your vision.

Amen.

January 2

In the time of King Herod, after Jesus was born in Bethlehem of Judea, wise men from the East came to Jerusalem, asking, "Where is the child who has been born king of the Jews? For we observed his star at its rising, and have come to pay him homage."

Matthew 2:1–2

"Why didn't you ask for directions?" a supervisor once asked me. Reflecting on how confident I was when I began, I could only say, "I didn't know that I didn't know." I am a better question-asker now. Our Scripture today has wise men asking for directions to remind all of us to ask more questions on our journeys through life.

Understanding God, give us confidence in ourselves tempered with wisdom so that we can be better servants to your kingdom.

Amen.

January 3

*On entering the house, they saw the child with Mary
his mother; and they knelt down and paid him homage.
Then opening their treasure chests, they offered him
gifts of gold, frankincense, and myrrh. And having
been warned in a dream not to return to Herod, they
left for their own country by another road.*

MATTHEW 2:11–12

The wise men listened to a dream and went
home by another road, saving the infant Jesus.
While I can't say I have ever received directions in
a dream from God, I do know that hearing God's
voice in my own life has taken patience, effort, and
the willingness to take a road not originally planned
at times.

*Gracious God, grant us discernment
so that we are able to comprehend
more clearly your plan for us.*

Amen.

January 4

*Thus says God, the L*ORD*, who created the heavens and stretched them out, who spread out the earth and what comes from it, who gives breath to the people upon it and spirit to those who walk in it.*

ISAIAH 42:5

God created us as spirit-filled beings. When our bodies are sick, our spirits are affected, and when our spirits ache, we often have physical manifestations of that pain. In caring for ourselves, we must be mindful of this and offer ourselves whole-person care.

Creator God, help us better care for both our bodies and our spirits.

Amen.

January 5

*And when Jesus had been baptized, just as he came
up from the water, suddenly the heavens were
opened to him and he saw the Spirit of God
descending like a dove and alighting on him. And
a voice from heaven said, "This is my Son, the
Beloved, with whom I am well pleased."*

MATTHEW 3:16–17

Throughout my life, I have been associated with denominations that practice infant baptism. In most infant baptisms, a significant part of the service occurs when the adult members of the congregation agree to assist the parents in raising the child in the faith. At that moment, all members of the congregation take responsibility for the faith development of each other and especially of the children.

*Gracious God, keep us mindful that all whom
we see today are your children.*

Amen.

January 6

I am the Lord, I have called you in righteousness, I have taken you by the hand and kept you; I have given you as a covenant to the people, a light to the nations, to open the eyes that are blind, to bring out the prisoners from the dungeon, from the prison those who sit in darkness.

Isaiah 42:6–7

These directions intimately tie physical healing ("open the eyes that are blind") with hope ("bring out the prisoners from the dungeon"). This passage asks for action from us. Consider how your actions today might bring further healing and hope to all around you.

Gracious God, you ask us to offer healing and hope to those who come to us. Help us today and every day in this wonderful endeavor of love.

Amen.

January 7

For he delivers the needy when they call, the poor and those who have no helper. He has pity on the weak and the needy, and saves the lives of the needy.

PSALM 72:12–13

I consider myself a helper to my wife, children and parents. Yet, I am old enough that I am beginning to worry about who will help me later in life. Many people in life have no one to help them. Consider who helps you today and how you might help others, especially those in great need.

Caring God, be our guide as we seek to be helpers to those around us. And when we need assistance, send helpers to us.

Amen.

January 8

A leper came to him begging him, and kneeling he
said to him, "If you choose, you can make me
clean." Moved with pity, Jesus stretched out his
hand and touched him, and said to him, "I do
choose. Be made clean!"

MARK 1:40–42

Jesus not only healed the leper but also restored
his relationship with both God and his community.
For Jesus, healing was both an act of curing and an
act of restoration.

Almighty God, help us be restorative presences
for those around us today.

Amen.

January 9

*Or do you not know that your body is a temple of the
Holy Spirit within you, which you have from God, and
that you are not your own? For you were bought with
a price; therefore glorify God in your body.*

1 CORINTHIANS 6:19–20

Ome of my favorite benedictions begins: "As you
leave this place and go out into the world …"
I have also heard pastors dismiss congregations
with a line similar to this: "May ministry begin …"
Prayer and discernment are necessary, but we have
to translate that into bodily action and service.

*Understanding God, help us this and
every day to walk our talk.*

Amen.

January 10

*Now there are varieties of gifts, but the same Spirit;
and there are varieties of services, but the same Lord;
and there are varieties of activities, but it is the same
God who activates all of them in everyone.*

1 CORINTHIANS 12:4–6

We have different schedules and job descriptions. We have different skill sets among us. Despite our differences, we are reminded that God is at the center of all we do. Whatever our gifts, each of us serves God in the work we do.

*Almighty God, bless our efforts as we
try to use the gifts you have given us to
better your kingdom.*

Amen.

January 11

*To each is given the manifestation of the
Spirit for the common good.*

1 CORINTHIANS 12:7

Our gifts from God are not secret skills God
grants to us for personal use. Our gifts are "for
the common good." Consider for a moment today
if you are sharing your gifts to the fullest.

*Gracious God, help us to share more willingly
our gifts with one another.*

Amen.

January 12

*For it was you who formed my inward parts; you knit
me together in my mother's womb. I praise you, for I
am fearfully and wonderfully made. Wonderful are
your works; that I know very well.*

PSALM 139:13–14

Do you ever get down on yourself? I am my own
worst critic, and I can be terribly hard on
myself. While this trait can be creatively helpful at
times, providing drive and motivation, it can also
be disabling to me. Be reminded today that each of
us is an amazing work of art in God's gallery here
on earth.

*Creator God, you have made us in your image.
Help us embrace that in ourselves and in all of
those around us today.*

Amen.

January 13

Love is patient; love is kind ... love rejoices in the truth. It bears all things, believes all things, hopes all things, endures all things. Love never ends.

1 CORINTHIANS 13:4, 6–8

Our daily work at the Church Health Center helps people through challenging journeys toward health and wellness. We strive to be patient, kind, and respectful of each individual's worth as a child of God. We deliver good medicine and good science with ample doses of love.

Steadfast God, be with each of us as we serve your children today.

Amen.

January 14

Then I said, "Here I am; in the scroll of the book it is written of me. I delight to do your will, O my God; your law is within my heart."

PSALM 40:7–8

The psalmist exclaims that in the scroll it will be written: "I have made myself available to do your will, O my God." The psalmist goes on to write that he doesn't hide God's love, righteousness, and faithfulness in his heart. Rather, he shares it freely with those around him "in the great assembly."

Almighty God, strengthen us so that we might learn from the psalmist to do your will boldly.

Amen.

January 15

Beloved, let us love one another,
because love is from God; everyone who
loves is born of God and knows God.

1 JOHN 4:7

Rev. Dr. Martin Luther King, Jr. spoke of the day when we would live in the beloved community. In Colossians 3:14 love is described as binding everything together in perfect harmony. I believe that God asks us, as people of faith, to act in ways that move us toward the realization of this dream of the beloved community.

Loving God, help us as we work in numerous
ways to create a beloved community
at home and in the world.

Amen.

January 16

*Praise the LORD! I will give thanks to the LORD
with my whole heart, in the company of the
upright, in the congregation.*

PSALM 111:1

One way people praise God with their whole
hearts is by adding movement to their prayers.
Consider today a way to add movement to your
regular prayer time.

*Gracious God, open our minds
to new ways to praise you.*

Amen.

January 17

*The heavens are telling the glory of God; and the
firmament proclaims his handiwork. Day to day pours
forth speech, and night to night declares knowledge.*

PSALM 19:1–2

Do you want to find God? This passage reminds
us that finding God is as simple as looking
around you—at the wonder of creation, at the cry
of a small child, at the glorious day that we too often
take for granted.

*Creator God, help our eyes see you as wind
blows through our hair, as rain falls on our
face and as a new friend smiles at us.*

Amen.

January 18

Now I appeal to you, brothers and sisters, by the name of our Lord Jesus Christ, that all of you should be in agreement and that there should be no divisions among you, but that you should be united in the same mind and the same purpose.

1 CORINTHIANS 1:10

The Church Health Center is a mission-driven organization. We talk about our mission frequently because we want to be united in the same mind and the same purpose even amidst the great diversity of our staff. But this is a call to all people of faith, and not just to those of us who are members of a particular organization.

God who loves us all, be with us each day as we seek to reclaim the mission of your church to care for people in both body and spirit.

Amen.

January 19

As Jesus went from there, he saw two other brothers,
James son of Zebedee and his brother John, in the
boat with their father Zebedee, mending their nets,
and he called them. Immediately they left the boat
and their father, and followed him.

MATTHEW 4:21–22

Jesus called them. People of faith talk a lot about
being called—missing your calling and fulfilling
your calling. What we often miss is that to hear God
calling, we have to be listening. For me, calling is
about developing an attitude of listening—listening
for that still small voice of God.

Loving God, help us to be better listeners in all
aspects of our lives. Help us hear each other,
but also help us hear you so that we might
know your will for us.

Amen.

January 20

Are all apostles? Are all prophets? Are all teachers?
Do all work miracles? Do all possess gifts of healing?
Do all speak in tongues? Do all interpret?
But strive for the greater gifts.

1 CORINTHIANS 12:29–31

And what are those greater gifts? Immediately following this passage is 1 Corinthians 13, where the greater gifts are faith, hope, and love. Along with honoring gifts such as teaching or healing, let us strive toward those greater gifts together.

Loving God, deepen our faith, raise our hope,
and increase our capacity to love.

Amen.

January 21

"Will the Lord be pleased with thousands of rams, with ten thousands of rivers of oil? Shall I give my firstborn for my transgression, the fruit of my body for the sin of my soul?" He has told you, O mortal, what is good; and what does the Lord require of you but to do justice, and to love kindness, and to walk humbly with your God?

MICAH 6:7–8

We live not as islands but as people in community. The prophet tells us that how we care for one another matters more than empty ritual.

Almighty God, bless our efforts as we seek to do your will among our brothers and sisters.

Amen.

January 22

*Blessed are the peacemakers, for they will
be called children of God.*

MATTHEW 5:9

Peace is so often thought of as the absence of war,
but peace also includes cooperating with and
considering the needs of others. We strive for peace
in the workplace, where it is important to remember
that we are working together toward God's plan
and not ours.

*Loving God, help us keep the
main thing, the main thing.*

Amen.

January 23

*Then I said, "Ah, Lord GOD! Truly I do not know how
to speak, for I am only a boy." But the LORD said to
me, "Do not say, 'I am only a boy'; for you shall go to
all to whom I send you, and you shall speak whatever I
command you. Do not be afraid of them for I am with
you to deliver you, says the LORD."*

JEREMIAH 1:6–8

We may not be prophets like Jeremiah, but this
passage reminds me of the importance of
listening carefully to God's conversation in our lives.

*Gracious God, help our ears better hear and
our souls better understand the conversation
you are having with us.*

Amen.

January 24

*When you reap the harvest of your land, you shall
not reap to the very edges of your field, or gather
the gleanings of your harvest. You shall not strip
your vineyard bare, or gather the fallen grapes of
your vineyard; you shall leave them for the poor
and the alien: I am the LORD your God.*

LEVITICUS 19:9–10

This passage instructs us to consider the needs
of those less fortunate than we are. We are
supposed to give to "the poor and the alien" not
simply that which misses our harvest buckets but
some of the first fruits of our labor. To share with
others we have first to allow nature to replenish
itself, taking only what we need and conserving our
resources for the next generation.

*Gracious God, bless our work offered to others
this day. May all our efforts be our best efforts.*

Amen.

January 25

*Since, then, we have such hope, we act with great
boldness. ... Now the Lord is the Spirit, and where the
Spirit of the Lord is, there is freedom. And all of us,
with unveiled faces, seeing the glory of the Lord as
though reflected in a mirror, are being transformed
into the same image from one degree of glory to
another; for this comes from the Lord, the Spirit.
Therefore, since it is by God's mercy that we are
engaged in this ministry, we do not lose heart.*

2 CORINTHIANS 3:12; 17–4:1

We have seen the unveiled glory of God in the
person of Jesus Christ, and we believe that
the Spirit of God dwells in each of us. Called by
God. Led by God. Emboldened by God.

*Almighty God, help us to live more confidently
knowing that you are dwelling inside us.*

Amen.

January 26

Jesus said to them, "Fill the jars with water." And they
filled them up to the brim. He said to them, "Now
draw some out, and take it to the chief steward." So
they took it. When the steward tasted the water
that had become wine …

JOHN 2:7–9

I n the Gospel of John, Jesus has been baptized, has
selected disciples, and now is attending a wedding
in Cana. This turning of the water into wine is Jesus'
first recorded miracle. It is often read during
Epiphany because it is considered the first revelation
of Jesus' divine prerogative to perform miracles.

Almighty God, you grant each of us gifts.
Reveal those gifts to us so that we can use
them in ways that build up your kingdom.

Amen.

January 27

Is this not the fast that I choose: to loose the bonds
of injustice, to undo the thongs of the yoke, to let
the oppressed go free, and to break every yoke? Is it
not to share your bread with the hungry, and
bring the homeless poor into your house; when you
see the naked, to cover them, and not to hide
yourself from your own kin?

ISAIAH 58:6−7

We are approaching the season of Lent when many Christians will consider some sort of fast. When done for the right reasons, fasts can help the participant feel a closer connection to God. These verses remind us that an important way to live in closer communion with God is by taking care of one another, especially those less fortunate than we are.

Gracious God, guide us to be better sharers of
the abundance you have provided.

Amen.

January 28

When I was a child, I spoke like a child, I thought like a child, I reasoned like a child; when I became an adult, I put an end to childish ways. For now we see in a mirror, dimly, but then we will see face to face. Now I know only in part; then I will know fully, even as I have been fully known. And now faith, hope and love abide, these three; and the greatest of these is love.

1 CORINTHIANS 13:11–13

Through the years my faith has taught me to be comfortable with not knowing all the answers. I've grown into living with questions. That leaves me walking in a journey of faith that gives me hope and that directs me to try hard each day to love my neighbor as I love myself.

Loving God, thank you for accompanying us on this journey of faith. May our journey draw us closer to you.

Amen.

January 29

"Food will not bring us close to God." We are no
worse off if we do not eat, and no better off if we do.
But take care that this liberty of yours does not
somehow become a stumbling block to the weak.

1 CORINTHIANS 8:8–9

"**D**o no harm," is part of the oath of new
physicians, and this Scripture seems to be
saying the same thing to us in our dealings with
each other on matters of faith.

Merciful God, help us nurture the faith
of all those we see today.

Amen.

January 30

He gives power to the faint, and strengthens the powerless. Even youths will faint and be weary, and the young will fall exhausted; but those who wait for the LORD shall renew their strength, they shall mount up with wings like eagles, they shall run and not be weary, they shall walk and not faint.

ISAIAH 40:29–31

I always think of Bette Midler's "Wind Beneath My Wings" when I hear this Scripture. She sings of the devoted and supportive friend who is always there for her. I like to think of God as such a friend, who loves us despite our shortcomings.

Steadfast God, help us remember that we cannot soar in this world without your presence and your help.

Amen.

January 31

*Now concerning food sacrificed to idols: we know that
"all of us possess knowledge." Knowledge puffs up, but
love builds up. Anyone who claims to know something
does not yet have the necessary knowledge; but anyone
who loves God is known by him.*

1 Corinthians 8:1–3

There are two related ideas in this powerful message: first, we must be careful in our dealings with each other on matters of faith because our own knowledge is incomplete. Second, we must realize that even though our knowledge is incomplete, God loves us and knows us.

*God of mystery, we have so many questions
yet you love us anyway.
Thank you for your faith in us.*

Amen.

February

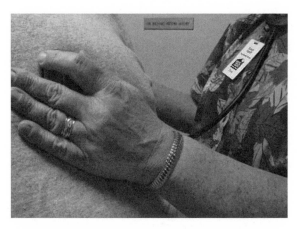

A check-up in the Church Health Center Clinic.

February 1

And even if our gospel is veiled, it is veiled to those who are perishing. In their case the god of this world has blinded the minds of the unbelievers, to keep them from seeing the light of the gospel of the glory of Christ, who is the image of God.

2 CORINTHIANS 4:3–4

I have known individuals who come to church as spiritually damaged people, sometimes finding it difficult to see fully the light of God. I hope and pray that as we work together, our collective light can shine brightly enough to pierce the veils these neighbors are wearing.

Merciful God, help each of us be a light for the world by being a light for the person sitting in front of us today.

Amen.

February 2

The LORD will guide you continually, and satisfy your needs in parched places, and make your bones strong; and you shall be like a watered garden, like a spring of water, whose waters never fail. Your ancient ruins shall be rebuilt; you shall raise up the foundations of many generations; you shall be called the repairer of the breach, the restorer of the streets to live in.

ISAIAH 58:11–12

These verses bring us full circle. As we care for one another, we also bring healing to our world. Each of us becomes a "repairer of the breach" and a "restorer of the streets." When we look for ways to restore our own bodies and spirits, we become more aware of our environment and more appreciative of the interdependence of all living beings in this world.

Creator God, bless our individual efforts to bring healing to one another.

Amen.

February 3

*Just then there was in their synagogue a man with
an unclean spirit, and he cried out, "What have you
to do with us, Jesus of Nazareth? Have you come to
destroy us? I know who you are, the Holy One of
God." But Jesus rebuked him, saying, "Be silent,
and come out of him!" And the unclean spirit,
throwing him into convulsions and crying with a
loud voice came out of him.*

MARK 1:23–26

Jesus healed people everywhere he went. He
healed on the Sabbath and in synagogues—a
source of his problems among the religious leaders
of his day. But Jesus sets an example here and in
other Scriptures that sends a clear message: healing
is paramount to his and our ministries.

*Almighty God, help us be healing
presences to people at all times.*

Amen.

February 4

And so, brothers and sisters, I could not speak to you as spiritual people, but rather as people of the flesh, as infants in Christ. I fed you with milk, not solid food, for you were not ready for solid food.

1 CORINTHIANS 3:1–2

I take comfort in passages such as this one. Paul is acknowledging that the Corinthians are people of faith, but their faith journey, like ours, is one of becoming more deeply connected to God over time.

Steadfast God, may our faith in you, our understanding of you, grow deeper today and every day.

Amen.

February 5

*Then your light shall break forth like the dawn, and
your healing shall spring up quickly; your
vindicator shall go before you, the glory of the Lord
shall be your rearguard.*

Isaiah 58:8

This verse follows Isaiah's admonition to loosen
the bonds of injustice, share bread with the
poor and bring the homeless into your home (verses
6–8). We find our healing through helping others
heal. We find our light by helping others' light
shine through.

*Almighty God, we ask your blessings as
we seek to do your will through the holy
work of helping others.*

Amen.

February 6

So neither the one who plants nor the one who waters is anything, but only God who gives the growth. The one who plants and the one who waters have a common purpose ... For we are God's servants, working together; you are God's field, God's building.

1 CORINTHIANS 3:7–9

We are the body of Christ. We are on the same team, but as individual team members, we have different roles to play. Together we are working toward the common purpose of fulfilling God's will.

Almighty God, work within and among us so that this world will become as you envision it.

Amen.

February 7

You are the light of the world. A city built on a hill cannot be hidden. No one after lighting a lamp puts it under a bushel basket, but on the lampstand, and it gives light to all in the house. In the same way, let your light shine before others, so that they may see your good works and give glory to your Father in heaven.

<small>MATTHEW 5:14–16</small>

Through our care for one another, our light shines. As people of faith, we should care for one another. Consider the beacon we create for others when we all work together.

Everlasting God, bless our individual acts of mercy and healing. May the flicker of our own lights thus created combine in ways that bathe others in your light.

Amen.

February 8

You shall not hate in your heart anyone of your kin … You shall not take vengeance or bear a grudge against any of your people, but you shall love your neighbor as yourself: I am the Lord.

LEVITICUS 19:17–18

"Love your neighbor as yourself" is surely one of the most recognized phrases in Scripture. The Golden Rule, or the ethic of reciprocity as it is also called, is found in some form in nearly every world religion. This rule by which we strive to live provides us a common reference point for all people of faith.

Almighty God, help us better recognize our neighbors and treat them as we would like to be treated.

Amen.

February 9

For Simon Peter and all who were with him were
amazed at the catch of fish that they had taken; and so
also were James and John, sons of Zebedee, who were
partners with Simon. Then Jesus said to Simon, "Do
not be afraid; from now on you will be catching
people." When they had brought their boats to shore,
they left everything and followed him.

LUKE 5:9–11

Jesus recruited ordinary fishermen, who had good days and bad days and days when God filled their nets to capacity, to carry out his three-fold directive to preach, teach and heal. Jesus chose patient laborers to learn at his feet and to carry his message to us. Consider today how you are being called to proclaim God's kingdom.

Gracious God, grant us a portion of the
faith of these fishermen so that we can
follow you more closely.

Amen.

February 10

I give you thanks, O LORD, with my whole heart;
before the gods I sing your praise; For though the LORD
is high, he regards the lowly; but the haughty he
perceives from far away.

PSALM 138:1, 6

A favorite prayer ending I have heard: "In the name of the one who sits on high but reaches down low. Amen." My prayer is that your work today, whatever work that is, touches someone who otherwise would not have been helped.

Loving God, be with us in our daily
walk with you. Help us better know
the needs of our neighbors.

Amen.

February 11

*Now there are varieties of gifts, but the same Spirit;
and there are varieties of services, but the same Lord;
and there are varieties of activities, but it is the same
God who activates all of them in everyone.*

1 CORINTHIANS 12:4–6

I am comforted knowing that God has worked in each of us and that each of us has been blessed with gifts to offer one another. My prayer is that each of us will find, claim, and use the gifts God gives.

*Loving God, give us the vision to discern more
clearly our gifts so that we can better live into
your vision of us.*

Amen.

February 12

Blessed are the merciful, for they will receive mercy.
MATTHEW 5:7

A wise manager of mine once told me that most people treat others as they wish to be treated themselves. Reflect on this idea throughout the day as you interact with others and consider the message you are sending with your actions.

Merciful God, help us as we seek to be caregivers for one another.

Amen.

February 13

The LORD is my light and my salvation; whom shall I fear? The LORD is the stronghold of my life; of whom shall I be afraid?

PSALM 27:1

I sometimes feel as though my life is being filmed, and my actions are being judged by all around me. This can create an unintentional timidity. Psalm 27 reminds us that God strengthens us in our daily life, and we should move boldly into the days ahead of us, serving God to the best of our ability.

Almighty God, help us walk assured of your love and support.

Amen.

February 14

The Lord said to Moses, "Come up to me on the mountain, and wait there; and I will give you the tablets of stone.

Exodus 24:12

I have trouble imagining the vastness of God, so I like that Moses had to go to a mountaintop to see God. I was once at the summit of Pikes Peak in Colorado where I was able to see not only all of Colorado but also several surrounding states. This experience helped me to envision the magnitude of God.

Ever-present God, help us to remember that wherever we are, you are already there.

Amen.

February 15

*Now about eight days after these sayings Jesus took
with him Peter and John and James, and went up on
the mountain to pray. And while he was praying, the
appearance of his face changed, and his clothes became
dazzling white ... they saw his glory.*

LUKE 9:28–29, 32

Most of us won't see Jesus in such glory while
we are alive. But all of us need mountaintop
experiences for our faith from time to time.

*Loving God, thank you for those precious
mountaintop experiences that refresh and
inspire us for the work ahead of us.*

Amen.

February 16

Just as they were leaving him, Peter said to Jesus, "Master, it is good for us to be here; let us make three dwellings, one for you, one for Moses, and one for Elijah"—not knowing what he said.

LUKE 9:33

"Can't we stay a little longer?" There is comfort in what is known, so it isn't surprising that Peter would want the moment of the Transfiguration to last. But life is lived in community with others, and we must trust that God remains by our side as we walk down our own hills into the unknown that lies before us.

Loving God, we spend most of our time on the plain trying to do your will. Thank you for your steadfast presence.

Amen.

February 17

*If you remove the yoke from among you, the
pointing of the finger, the speaking of evil, if you
offer food to the hungry and satisfy the needs of the
afflicted, then your light shall rise in the darkness
and your gloom be like the noonday.*

ISAIAH 58:9–10

Our lights shine as we help others' lights shine, but this passage asks that we "satisfy the needs of the afflicted." Determining the actual needs of our neighbors, however, is quite difficult. Feeding someone is easy. Feeding someone a nutritious, healthy meal requires intentionality, forethought and willingness.

*Gracious and merciful God, help us
understand the true needs of our neighbors so
our help may satisfy the needs you see.*

Amen.

February 18

"When you fast, put oil on your head and wash your face, so that your fasting may be seen not by others but by your Father who is in secret; and your Father who sees in secret will reward you."

MATTHEW 6:17–18

The fast we are asked to choose is one which looks deeply at the needs of our neighbors. It is a fast aimed at justice for all rather than denial of self. It is a fast that pierces the dark places of our world. It is a fast that places priorities in the right order.

Gracious and merciful God, the fast we choose requires your lead. Take our hands.

Amen.

February 19

Now when the Lord was about to take Elijah up to heaven by a whirlwind, Elijah and Elisha were on their way from Gilgal. Elijah said to Elisha, "Stay here; for the Lord has sent me as far as Bethel." But Elisha said, "As the Lord lives, and as you yourself live, I will not leave you." So they went down to Bethel.

2 Kings 2:1–2

I am fortunate to have several Elishas in my life—family and friends who would stay with me no matter what. Think of Elishas in your life today, and give thanks to God for them.

Loving God, thank you for those people in our lives on whom we can count to be with us through all of life's ups and downs. Help us be better Elishas in their lives, too.

Amen.

February 20

Therefore I tell you, do not worry about your life, what you will eat or what you will drink, or about your body, what you will wear. Is not life more than food, and the body more than clothing?

MATTHEW 6:25

Our founder and executive director, Rev. Dr. Scott Morris, often reminds us that life for life's sake isn't worth much. To encourage one to quit smoking simply to add a few years to one's life rarely offers sufficient motivation. He goes on to say that what makes life worth living are those things that drive us closer to God, such as more joy and love.

Gracious God, help us first seek those things which draw us closer to you, which allow you easier passage into our hearts.

Amen.

February 21

For there is no distinction between Jew and Greek;
the same Lord is Lord of all and is generous to all
who call on him. For, "Everyone who calls on the
name of the Lord shall be saved."

ROMANS 10:12–13

For most, the walk toward health is filled with both success and failure. Unfortunately, the failures often create obstacles that prevent us from restarting. Love yourself as God loves you.

Loving God, you accept us as we are.
Help us better accept ourselves.

Amen.

February 22

*But our citizenship is in heaven, and it is from there
that we are expecting a Savior, the Lord Jesus
Christ. He will transform the body of our
humiliation that it may be conformed to the body of
his glory, by the power that also enables him to make
all things subject to himself.*

PHILIPPIANS 3:20–21

Self-image can be a help or a hindrance in the
journey toward healthier living. Paul admonishes
us to be proud of our shared heritage as children
of heaven, reminding us that we are the body of
Christ first.

*Sovereign God, help us take better care of
ourselves, keeping us mindful that there is no
shame in Christ's body.*

Amen.

February 23

The devil said to him, "If you are the Son of God,
command this stone to become a loaf of bread."
Jesus answered him, "It is written, 'One does
not live by bread alone.'"

Luke 4:3–4

Quick fixes dominate our culture. The spiritual journey requires time and patience. Pause to take in spiritual sustenance, to proclaim personal Sabbath time. Living abundantly requires regular eating from the spiritual food group, too.

God of abundance, help us consume the
spiritual nourishment you freely offer us.

Amen.

February 24

Ho, everyone who thirsts, come to the waters; and you
that have no money, come, buy and eat! Come, buy
wine and milk without money and without price. Why
do you spend your money for that which is not bread,
and your labor for that which does not satisfy? Listen
carefully to me, and eat what is good, and delight
yourselves in rich food.

ISAIAH 55:1–2

A wine taster, who holds the wine glass up to the light, swirls and sniffs the wine then savors a sip. In doing this, the essence of the wine is uncovered, its complexities discovered. Likewise may we savor God's Word.

Almighty God, help us taste your Word so
that it nourishes us as you desire.

Amen.

February 25

Then the devil led Jesus up and showed him in an
instant all the kingdoms of the world. And the devil
said to him, "To you I will give their glory and all this
authority; for it has been given over to me, and I give it
to anyone I please. If you, then, will worship me, it
will all be yours." Jesus answered him, "It is written,
'Worship the Lord your God, and serve only him.'"

LUKE 4:5–8

Temptation, whether obvious or insidious, is a
challenging part of living. How one handles
temptation, through strength of character and
forgiveness of self, in large part will determine
one's success.

Forgiving God, help us better forgive
ourselves, as you have already forgiven us.

Amen.

February 26

Is this not the fast I choose: to loose the bonds of injustice, to undo the thongs of the yoke, to let the oppressed go free, and to break every yoke? Is it not to share bread with the hungry, and bring the homeless poor into your house; when you see the naked, to cover them, and not to hide yourself from your own kin?

ISAIAH 58:6–7

Fasting is a common observance during Lent, although not one in which I have regularly participated. While we can pay honor to and reflect on God through fasting, this passage reminds us that we also serve God through our service to others each day.

Gracious God, help us share ourselves with others in ways which are pleasing to you.

Amen.

February 27

*Make me to know your ways, O LORD; teach me
your paths. Lead me in your truth, and teach
me, for you are the God of my salvation; for you
I wait all day long.*

PSALM 25:4–5

When I read these three verses, I thought of the
hymn "Here I Am, Lord." The songwriter
reminds us to listen for God's call and go where
God leads. I think these verses make a wonderful
prayer for each day, but they are especially
meaningful during Lent.

*God of the day and the night, open our ears to
hear your call and our hearts to follow you.*

Amen.

February 28

And the Spirit immediately drove him out into the
wilderness. He was in the wilderness forty days,
tempted by Satan; and he was with the wild beasts;
and the angels waited on him.

MARK 1:12–13

Following his baptism, Jesus went into the wilderness. We symbolically venture into the wilderness for forty days during Lent, a season that leads to Easter and the Resurrection. It is my prayer that this season will be life-affirming for each of you.

Steadfast God, thank you for walking beside us
each day. Help us to know your true voice so
that we won't be distracted along the way.

Amen.

February 29

You who fear the LORD, praise him! All you offspring of Jacob, glorify him; stand in awe of him, all you offspring of Israel! For he did not despise or abhor the affliction of the afflicted; he did not hide his face from me, but heard when I cried to him.

PSALM 22:23–24

Each week at the Church Health Center, we hold a prayer service where employees, patients, and members pray for the healing of themselves and others. Throughout Scripture as in this Psalm, we are assured that God doesn't turn from us in our times of need and that God hears our prayers.

Healing God, we thank you for your steadfast, healing presence in our lives and for hearing both our spoken and unspoken prayers.

Amen.

March

*Class training to be Congregational
Health Promoters.*

March 1

Jesus asked them, "Do you think that because these Galileans suffered in this way they were worse sinners than all other Galileans? No, I tell you; but unless you repent, you will all perish as they did."

LUKE 13:2–3

Whether intentionally or unintentionally, we often make value judgments on those who are different from us. These value judgments often cloud our view of those left out of the systems of support we have in areas like access to health care or housing. Yet, the Jewish word for repent, *teshuvah*, means simply return to God—return to the God whose steadfast love includes abundant pardon.

Steadfast God, help our journeys in life always to move toward you.

Amen.

March 2

*From now on, therefore, we regard no one from a
human point of view; even though we once knew
Christ from a human point of view, we know him
no longer in that way. So if anyone is in Christ,
there is a new creation: everything old has passed
away; see everything has become new!*

2 CORINTHIANS 5:16–17

It is easy to look at a person as a gender or a skin
color or as a member of a certain socioeconomic
class. We ascribe values and prejudices to these and
other traits. But as people of faith, we are called to
look at people through God's lens.

*Loving God, remove the scales of prejudice
and presumption from our eyes so that we
might see people as you do.*

Amen.

March 3

You shall not make for yourself an idol,
whether in the form of anything that is in
heaven above, or that is on the earth beneath,
or that is in the water under the earth.

EXODUS 20:4

My handheld, e-mail-checking, schedule-reminding telephone remains glued to my side at all times. Some would say my coffee cup is as attached to me, too. Let us consider today the idols we have erected in our lives.

Understanding God, while we may not have
golden calves erected as objects of worship in
our lives, we do have obstacles blocking our
ability to live in full relationship with you.
Give us the wisdom to recognize these barriers
and the courage to remove them.

Amen.

March 4

In the temple he found people selling cattle, sheep, and doves, and the money changers seated at their tables. Making a whip of cords, he drove all of them out of the temple, both the sheep and the cattle. He also poured out the coins of the money changers and overturned their tables. He also told those who were selling the doves, "Takes these things out of here! Stop making my Father's house a market-place!"

JOHN 2:14–16

I t is embarrassing when I consider how many opinions I make of people by superficial things like clothes worn, car driven, restaurant frequented, or degrees earned. Each of us is a child of God, wholly and equally loved. Today's Scripture pulls at this tension between the worldly and the spiritual.

Creator God, we are yours. Help us live together as the brothers and sisters we are.

Amen.

March 5

*On the day after the passover, on that very
day, they ate the produce of the land,
unleavened cakes and parched grain.*

JOSHUA 5:11

A localvore is a person dedicated to eating food
grown and produced locally. Food from
within your region needs fewer preservatives to
maintain freshness and uses less fossil fuel in
delivering the product to you, making it healthier
for you and the planet. Let us all eat "the produce
of the land" this day.

*Bounteous God, for lush fields,
succulent fruits, and hearty
grains, we give you thanks today.*

Amen.

March 6

As God's chosen ones, holy and beloved,
clothe yourselves with compassion, kindness,
humility, meekness, and patience.
COLOSSIANS 3:12

This passage is one of the guiding Scriptures we use at the Church Health Center. These virtues guide us in how we respond to and interact with our patients, members, donors and volunteers. Equally important, these virtues should dictate our actions toward one another.

Loving God, help us be the people
you want us to be.

Amen.

March 7

While I kept silence, my body wasted away through my groaning all day long. Therefore let all who are faithful offer prayer to you; at a time of distress, the rush of mighty waters shall not reach them.

PSALM 32:3, 6

Have you ever needed to cry but worked hard not to? Several times when this has happened to me, my throat has actually started hurting. This Scripture reminds us that holding "stuff" in can have both physical and spiritual manifestations. Today's Scripture could be rewritten in part to say, "Until I came to you in prayer, O God, my body was wracked with pain."

Wonderful, compassionate God, we value friends who are only a phone call away. Help us remember that you too are such a friend.

Amen.

March 8

Very truly, I tell you, unless a grain of wheat falls into the earth and dies, it remains just a single grain; but if it dies, it bears much fruit.

JOHN 12:24

Simply throwing seeds onto the ground generally yields less than gratifying results. If you want seeds to flourish, you must tend to their environment—the soil, the nutrients, the water. In a community sense, I see us as gardeners for one another, doing what we can so those around us can flourish.

Loving God, help us nurture one another in ways that help all of us to live abundantly.

Amen.

March 9

All this is from God, who reconciled us to himself through Christ, and has given us the ministry of reconciliation; that is, in Christ God was reconciling the world to himself, not counting their trespasses against them, and entrusting the message of reconciliation to us.

2 CORINTHIANS 5:18–19

Two synonyms for reconciliation are bringing together and understanding. I see my faith journey as a ministry that seeks to unite people. During your contemplative time today, consider your own ministry of reconciliation.

Gracious God, help us better understand your will so that we might be more help to others.

Amen.

March 10

Now the LORD said to Abram, "Go from your country and your kindred and your father's house to the land I will show you. I will make of you a great nation."

GENESIS 12:1–2

Abraham followed God on faith and became the father of three of the world's great religions—Judaism, Christianity, and Islam. So much separates us from each other. Today, rejoice in that which joins us together. Thanks, Father Abraham.

*Loving God of Abraham, help us
see each person placed before us
today as a brother or sister.*

Amen.

March 11

*So Jesus came to a Samaritan city called
Sychar ... and Jesus, tired out by his journey, was
sitting by the well. It was about noon. A Samaritan
woman came to draw water, and Jesus said to her,
"Give me a drink." ... The Samaritan woman said to
him, "How is it that you, a Jew, ask a drink of me,
a woman of Samaria?"*

JOHN 4:5–9

Jesus redefined neighbor to include not just "his
kind" but the whole of God's creation. If you are
given the opportunity today, risk showing God's
love to someone who makes you feel uncomfortable.

*Loving God, you ask us to see your face in
each person we meet. Help us to be faithful to
you in all our encounters.*

Amen.

March 12

Jesus said to her, "Go, call your husband, and come back." The woman answered him, "I have no husband." Jesus said to her, "You are right in saying, 'I have no husband'; for you have had five husbands, and the one you have now is not your husband. What you have said is true!" The woman said to him, "Sir, I see that you are a prophet."

JOHN 4:16–19

Ona of the enduring images offering direction to my faith is that of Jesus associating with the outcasts of his society. Each day we run into people whose pasts we do not know. Yet we are reminded through Scripture that all of them are children of our God.

Gentle God, help us as we seek to serve your children, our brothers and sisters. May they see your face in ours.

Amen.

March 13

He who vindicates me is near. Who will contend with me? Let us stand up together. Who are my adversaries? Let them confront me.

ISAIAH 50:8

People of faith: Stand Together! Throughout life, many of us struggle alone needlessly. God is always by our side, but often the best visual evidence of God's presence is when we stand together with our brothers and sisters of faith.

Loving God, help us create a community of faith where all of us feel supported and loved.

Amen.

March 14

"So he said to the gardener, 'See here! For three years I have come looking for fruit on this fig tree, and still I find none. Cut it down! Why should it be wasting this soil?' He replied, 'Sir, let it alone for one more year, until I dig around it and put manure on it.'"

LUKE 13:7–8

Gardens left unattended produce little. In our journeys toward God we are, like the gardener in the parable, fertilizing our faith. May all of our journeys produce abundant blooms and branches laden with fruit.

*Gracious, loving God, may your
Spirit well up inside us as we seek a
closer relationship with you.*

Amen.

March 15

The poor shall eat and be satisfied; those who seek him shall praise the LORD. May your hearts live forever! All the ends of the earth shall remember and turn to the LORD; and all the families of the nations shall worship before him.

PSALM 22:26–27

Our world can seem awfully unfriendly and unkind. This passage is a reminder that all of us are children of God, and our actions toward one another should come out of a real sense of familial love. When our poor brothers and sisters are hungry, we are called to act on behalf of God to help feed them.

Steadfast God, be with us in our daily struggle to do your will. Help us to live in faithful community with one another.

Amen.

March 16

The woman said to the serpent, "We may eat of
the fruit of the trees in the garden; but God said
'You shall not eat of the fruit of the tree that is in the
middle of the garden, nor shall you touch it, or you
shall die.'" But the serpent said to the woman, "You
will not die; for God knows that when you eat of it
your eyes will be opened, and you will be like God,
knowing good and evil."
GENESIS 3:2–5

Temptation confronts all of us. Broken resolutions
to ourselves and others provide all the evidence
we need of the power of temptation. But God stands
ready to provide support for our journey and
forgiveness for those times when we fall short.

Loving God, give us strength for each
day of our journey through life.
Be our guide. Be our beacon.

Amen.

March 17

"But when the younger son came to himself he said, 'How many of my father's hired hands have bread enough and to spare, but here I am dying of hunger! I will get up and go to my father, and I will say to him, "Father, I have sinned against heaven and before you; I am no longer worthy to be called your son; treat me like one of your hired hands."' So he set off and went to his father."

LUKE 15:17–20

Who do you see when you look at the face staring back at you in the mirror? Not only are we asked to look at others through God's lens, but we are also asked to look at ourselves in the same way. Before we can reconcile with God, we must first reconcile with ourselves.

*Parent God, just as you call us
to be gentle with one another,
help us be gentler with ourselves.*

Amen.

March 18

*I do not want you to be unaware, brothers and sisters,
that our ancestors were all under the cloud, and all
passed through the sea, and all were baptized into
Moses in the cloud and in the sea, and all ate the same
spiritual food, and all drank the same spiritual drink.
For they drank from the spiritual rock that followed
them, and the rock was Christ.*

1 CORINTHIANS 10:1–4

Paul, writing to the Corinthians about the Exodus,
goes on to remind them about the terrible things
that befell the Israelites with whom God was not
pleased (verse 5). This passage is a reminder that
while we might read similar Scriptures, our
interpretations can be vastly different. We need to
be gentle with one another remembering that God's
thoughts are not our thoughts.

*Gracious God, help us love and support
our neighbors as you desire.*

Amen.

March 19

*Jesus, knowing that the Father had given all things
into his hands, and that he had come from God and
was going to God, got up from the table, took off
his outer robe, and tied a towel around himself.
Then he poured water into a basin and began to
wash the disciples' feet and to wipe them with the
towel that was tied around him.*

JOHN 13:3–5

To wash someone's feet, both parties have to
become vulnerable to one another. A servant
to the end, Christ poured out his love for us. May
we be willing to risk allowing his intimate touch
in our lives.

*Understanding God, help us be more
vulnerable to your presence in our lives so that
we will walk closer to you.*

Amen.

March 20

*The glory of the L*ORD *settled on Mount Sinai, and
the cloud covered it for six days; on the seventh day,
he called to Moses out of the cloud. Now the
appearance of the glory of the L*ORD *was like a
devouring fire on the top of the mountain in the
sight of the people of Israel. Moses entered the cloud,
and went up on the mountain. Moses was on the
mountain for forty days and forty nights.*

EXODUS 24:16–18

We want our choices to be crystal clear, but they
rarely are. To approach God and receive the
law and commandments, Moses first had to walk
into a fog, where his vision would be limited and
his path uncertain. We are also asked by God to step
into the unknown on trust—to take a leap of faith.

*Mighty and wonderful God, strengthen our
faith so that we may boldly go where you lead.*

Amen.

March 21

As Jesus rode along, people kept spreading their cloaks on the road. As he was now approaching the path down from the Mount of Olives, the whole multitude of the disciples began to praise God joyfully with a loud voice for all the deeds of power that they had seen, saying, "Blessed is the king who comes in the name of the Lord! Peace in heaven, and glory in the highest heaven!"

LUKE 19:36–38

I t always makes me pause when I consider the fleetingness of human opinion, especially on important matters. The adoration of the crowds in today's passage will turn into disdain of the highest magnitude on Good Friday.

Steadfast God, strengthen my faith so that I might withstand the pull of the crowd away from you.

Amen.

March 22

*For by grace you have been saved through faith,
and this is not your own doing; it is the gift of
God—not the result of works, so that no one may
boast. For we are what he has made us, created in
Christ Jesus for good works, which God prepared
beforehand to be our way of life.*

Ephesians 2:8–10

Paul tells us that God created us for good works
to be our way of life—that our good works were
to be a natural outflow from our faith. It is humbling
to consider a world where all our actions toward
one another spring from our faith in God.

*Almighty God, work in us so we can be
the people you want us to be.*

Amen.

March 23

For once you were darkness, but now in the Lord you are light. Live as children of light—for the fruit of the light is found in all that is good and right and true.

EPHESIANS 5:8–9

I never grow weary of seeing lighthouses on the coast with lights so powerful as to cut through the thickest fog, so that ships can sail safely to port. As a child, I sang a church song that had a repeating line reminding us that the world will know we are Christians by our love. As people of faith, we are asked to be, in a sense, lighthouses of God's love.

God of Light, strengthen us so that we may be effective beacons of your love.

Amen.

March 24

*Then they brought the colt to Jesus and threw
their cloaks on it; and he sat on it. Many people
spread their cloaks on the road, and others
spread leafy branches that they had cut in the
fields. Then those who went ahead and those who
followed were shouting, "Hosanna! Blessed is
the one who comes in the name of the Lord!"*

MARK 11:7–9

The triumphal entry of Jesus into Jerusalem is a far cry from the heinous death he would suffer in a few days. If Jesus were among us today, would we give him honor, or would we see him as a radical? Would we be scared of his controversial views on religion, on love of neighbors, on love of enemies? Would we still be shouting hosannas at the end of the week?

*Steadfast God, thank you for
remaining faithful to us.*

Amen.

March 25

Blessed are you, O Lord; teach me your statutes.
With my lips I declare all the ordinances of your
mouth. I delight in the way of your decrees as much
as in all riches. I will meditate on your precepts, and
fix my eyes on your ways.

PSALM 119:12–15

I like the phrase "faith journey," because I think of my life as an ongoing conversation with God. Of course, as with any long conversation, I don't always listen as well as I should.

Gracious God, help us be better listeners to
your voice in our lives so that we can be more
like the people you want us to be.

Amen.

March 26

Seek the LORD while he may be found, call upon him while he is near; let the wicked forsake their way, and the unrighteous their thoughts; let them return to the LORD, that he may have mercy on them, and to our God, for he will abundantly pardon.

ISAIAH 55:6–7

Forgiveness can be difficult, and yet offering and receiving forgiveness can be an important step in one's journey toward healing. While forgiveness is hard for us, this passage assures that God not only forgives but does so abundantly.

Steadfast God, bless our efforts to do your will. Forgive the many times we fall short.

Amen.

March 27

*Create in me a clean heart, O God, and put a new
and right spirit within me. Do not cast me away
from your presence, and do not take your holy spirit
from me. Restore to me the joy of your salvation, and
sustain in me a willing spirit.*

PSALM 51:10–12

Throughout my life, my relationship with God has been on a continuum. Sometimes I have felt intimately connected to God, and at other times I have felt distanced from God. Of course at those times when I have felt farthest from God, I am the one who has been moving away.

*Steadfast God, thank you for
remaining faithful to us.*

Amen.

March 28

From Mount Hor they set out by the way to the
Red Sea, to go around the land of Edom; but the
people became impatient on the way. The people
spoke against God and against Moses, "Why have
you brought us up out of Egypt to die in the
wilderness? For there is no food and no water, and
we detest this miserable food."

NUMBERS 21:4–5

I s patience a virtue you have? Patience is one of
the virtues we strive for at the Church Health
Center, and yet patience is a work in progress for
most of us. This Scripture reminds us that we are
called to a patience that is grounded in radical trust
in God.

Almighty God, thank you for the patience you
have in us as we struggle toward a more
trusting relationship with you.

Amen.

March 29

Remember the sabbath day, and keep it holy. Six days you shall labor and do all your work. But the seventh day is a Sabbath to the LORD your God.

EXODUS 20:8–10

When it comes to our church leaders, one of the things that can be difficult to remember is that clergy need help with living a healthy life, too. People interested in clergy health are often concerned about clergy Sabbath-keeping, but in these times when many are holding onto two jobs, it is a question each of us should be asking ourselves. "Am I taking a day of rest? Am I making time to reconnect with God on a regular basis?"

Loving God, help us trust you more fully so that we can be better Sabbath-keepers.

Amen.

March 30

I am about to do a new thing; now it springs forth, do you not perceive it? I will make a way in the wilderness and rivers in the desert. The wild animals will honor me, the jackals and ostriches; for I give water in the wilderness, rivers in the desert, to give drink to my chosen people.

ISAIAH 43:19–20

I t is easy for us to place limits on God's power, but this passage reminds us that in God, the possibilities are limitless. Expect the unexpected. Expect the impossible, for we are walking into God's plan, not ours.

Almighty God, help us see the path toward which you are directing us.

Amen.

March 31

*Beloved, I do not consider that I have made it my
own; but this one thing I do: forgetting what lies
behind and straining forward to what lies ahead, I
press on toward the goal for the prize of the heavenly
call of God in Christ Jesus.*

PHILIPPIANS 3:13–14

Forget what lies behind you. What a powerfully
freeing line! Live as the forgiven person you are.
Live knowing that our God of endless possibilities
is not limited by our past so we aren't either.

*Gracious God, we have erected barriers
limiting our ability to follow your lead.
Help us to remove them.*

Amen.

April

Teaching in the Child Life area.

April 1

So the Jews gathered around and said to him, "How long will you keep us in suspense? If you are the Messiah, tell us plainly." Jesus answered, "I have told you, and you do not believe. The works that I do in my Father's name testify to me; but you do not believe because you do not belong to my sheep. My sheep hear my voice. I know them, and they follow me."

JOHN 10:24–27

I have read that shepherds often placed their sheep in a common pen at night. When the pen was opened the next morning, shepherds would call their sheep, and recognizing their master's voice, the sheep would follow the correct shepherd.

Almighty God, help us hear your voice more clearly.

Amen.

April 2

The hand of the LORD came upon me, and he
brought me out by the spirit of the LORD and set
me down in the middle of a valley; it was full of
bones. He led me all around them; there were very
many lying in the valley and they were very dry.
He said to me, "Mortal, can these bones live?" I
answered. "O Lord GOD you know." Then he said
to me, "Prophesy to these bones, and say to them:
O dry bones, hear the word of the LORD."

EZEKIEL 37:1–4

People often come to the Church Health Center when they are living in their own valley of dry bones, asking, in a way, "Can these bones live?" Then we begin the restorative work whether it's in the clinic or on the exercise court. Consider how you might offer healing to someone in need.

Loving God, help us be better
listeners for your voice.

Amen.

April 3

Jesus began to weep.
JOHN 11:35

When faced with the death of Lazarus, the grief of his sisters, and the struggles of the community of Bethany, Jesus was moved to tears. Christians speak of Jesus as fully human and fully divine. I ask you today to reflect on the fully human Jesus, whose love for Lazarus, Mary and Martha moved him to tears.

Gentle God, for each of us who experiences
a measure of sadness or disappointment
today, wrap loving arms around us
and give us comfort.

Amen.

April 4

When Jesus had said this, he cried with a loud voice, "Lazarus, come out!" The dead man came out, his hands and feet bound with strips of cloth, and his face wrapped in a cloth. Jesus said to them, "Unbind him, and let him go."

JOHN 11:43–44

In the raising of Lazarus, God answered Jesus' plea to release Lazarus from the shackles of death. While it is unlikely we will see someone raised from the dead in our lifetimes, our daily work as people of faith is, at least in part, to remove barriers that prevent people from living lives full of hope and healing.

Redeeming God, we seek to bring hope and healing to your children, our brothers and sisters. Be with us in this awesome task.

Amen.

April 5

Jesus got up from the table, took off his outer robe,
and tied a towel around himself. Then he poured
water into a basin and began to wash the disciples'
feet and to wipe them with the towel that was tied
around him ... "For I have set you an example, that
you also should do as I have done to you."

JOHN 13:4–5, 15

I think most of us want to do good, and we want
to help each other. But as I read these few verses,
I hear Jesus asking us to take service to one another
to a different level—to that of a servant. To help
someone is good, but to be a servant to another
requires a different attitude.

Gracious God, bless our efforts this
and every day as we seek to become
servants to one another.

Amen.

April 6

Now the whole group of those who believed were of one heart and soul, and no one claimed private ownership of any possessions, but everything they owned was held in common … There was not a needy person among them, for as many as owned lands or houses sold them and brought the proceeds of what was sold.

ACTS 4:32, 34

I am always proud of how we come together for one another after disasters like floods, tornadoes or hurricanes. This is where God helps us to see that we must be there for each other at all times.

Sustainer God, guide us in our efforts to help our neighbors when the need is obvious as well as when it is obscure.

Amen.

April 7

*When it was evening on that day, the first day of
the week, and the doors of the house where the
disciples had met were locked for fear of the Jews,
Jesus came and stood among them and said, "Peace
be with you." After he said this, he showed them
his hands and his side. Then the disciples rejoiced
when they saw the Lord.*

JOHN 20:19–20

When I read these lines, I tried to imagine what
it was like to be a disciple in those days
following the crucifixion. I am fairly certain I would
have been terrified for my life and gone behind
locked doors, too. I take comfort in knowing that
the people closest to Jesus were also scared, and
Jesus still appeared to them and had faith in them
to carry on his ministry.

*Almighty God, give us the strength needed to
meet any challenge we might face this day.*

Amen.

April 8

Jesus said to them again, "Peace be with you. As the
Father has sent me, so I send you." When he had
said this, he breathed on them and said to them,
"Receive the Holy Spirit."

John 20:21–22

I like the image connecting life-giving breath and the Holy Spirit in today's passage. Throughout the day, take moments to breathe in deeply. Imagine you are taking in the Holy Spirit with each breath, and treat each of these moments as a short prayer.

Almighty God, help us sense the
Holy Spirit within us each day.

Amen.

April 9

So Philip ran up to the Ethiopian eunuch and heard
him reading the prophet Isaiah. He asked, "Do you
understand what you are reading?" He replied, "How
can I, unless someone guides me?" And he invited
Philip to get in and sit beside him.

ACTS 8:30–31

The eunuch had trouble understanding Scripture
and asked Philip to help him with the
interpretation. Medical professionals are asked daily
to assist patients and clients in the interpretation of
their lab tests, health risks, medications and
prevention strategies. Like Philip's actions, these
actions can improve and even save lives—a privilege
not to be taken lightly.

Understanding God, regardless of our job
description, help us to understand our role as
interpreters for others who may need our
knowledge and understanding.

Amen.

April 10

*I keep the LORD always before me; because he is at
my right hand, I shall not be moved. Therefore my
heart is glad, and my soul rejoices; my body also
rests secure … You show me the path of life.*

PSALM 16:8–9, 11

Living in intimate relationship with God, the
psalmist experiences spiritual peace ("my soul
rejoices") and physical peace ("my body also rests
secure"). We work daily to live in closer relationship
with God, and at the Church Health Center we work
daily to help those who come to us to do the same.
Our paths of life are drawing us closer to God.

*Healer God, help us bring you into our lives
more deeply so we can live life more fully.*

Amen.

April 11

When the sabbath was over, Mary Magdalene,
and Mary the mother of James, and Salome bought
spices, so that they might go and anoint Jesus. And
very early on the first day of the week, when the
sun had risen, they went to the tomb. They had been
saying to one another, "Who will roll away the stone
for us from the entrance to the tomb?" When they
looked up, they saw that the stone, which was very
large, had already been rolled back.

MARK 16:1–4

Each one of us is an agent of resurrection. As we serve one another using our various gifts, we help others to find renewal and rebirth in their lives. We help to roll the stones away that are trapping them so that they can step out into new life.

Almighty God, we thank you for the gift of
Jesus, whose life provides guidance in how we
should serve and love you and one another.

Amen.

April 12

*How very good and pleasant it is when kindred
live together in unity! It is like the precious oil on
the head, running down upon the beard, on the
beard of Aaron, running down over the collar of
his robes. It is like the dew of Hermon, which falls
on the mountains of Zion. For there the LORD ordained
his blessing, life forevermore.*

PSALM 133:1–4

I n a land that can often be hot, dry, and parched,
Mt. Hermon rises to over 9,000 feet as the highest
peak in Israel. The water stored in its snow-capped
peaks is a vivid symbol of life to those looking up
from below. God wants and expects us to work
together in ways that are life-giving to one another.

*Gracious God, continue to lead us where
streams of living water flow.*

Amen.

April 13

We know love by this, that he laid down
his life for us—and we ought to lay
down our lives for one another.

1 JOHN 3:16

Would you die for a member of your family? I know many of you would immediately say, "Of course!" But would you die for your neighbor? Consider today what it means to live sacrificially for your neighbor, especially the neighbor who is actually a stranger.

Gracious God, many people will come in
contact with us today. Help us to see each of
them with your eyes.

Amen.

April 14

Saul got up from the ground, and though his eyes were open, he could see nothing; so they led him by the hand and brought him into Damascus. For three days he was without sight, and neither ate nor drank.

ACTS 9:8–9

Saul encounters Jesus in a dramatic way on the road to Damascus. Most of us won't be so fortunate. Listening for the still small voice of God requires intentionality, and yes, maybe even practice.

Almighty God, help us hear your will for us so that we can better serve you and your children.

Amen.

April 15

So Ananias went and entered the house. He laid his hands on Saul and said, "Brother Saul, the Lord Jesus, who appeared to you on your way here, has sent me so that you may regain your sight and be filled with the Holy Spirit." And immediately something like scales fell from his eyes, and his sight was restored.

ACTS 9:17–18

I think most of us suffer from spiritual blindness to varying degrees at different times in our life. While most of us won't meet Jesus in such a dramatic way in this life as Paul did, my prayer is that each of us will sense God's presence in palpable ways.

Steadfast God, help us sense your presence as we journey on our own roads to Damascus.

Amen.

April 16

But Thomas (who was called the Twin), one of the twelve, was not with them when Jesus came. So the other disciples told him, "We have seen the LORD." But he said to them, "Unless I see the mark of the nails in his hands, and put my finger in the mark of the nails and my hand in his side, I will not believe."

JOHN 20:24–25

I t is easy for most of us to relate to Doubting Thomas. The fact that Thomas doubted can help us feel more comfortable with our own questions— with the thinner places in our faith.

Steadfast God, we are on a faith journey and as with any journey, there are highs as well as lows. Thank you for always standing by us.

Amen.

April 17

And he will destroy on this mountain the shroud that is cast over all peoples, the sheet that is spread over all nations; he will swallow up death forever. Then the Lord God will wipe away the tears from all faces, and the disgrace of his people he will take away from all the earth, for the Lord has spoken.

ISAIAH 25:7–8

I love the image of God wiping away tears, and I hope each of you has had tears wiped from your face by someone who loves you. At my church, we say this line together each Sunday: "We will dry the tears of those who are weeping and know that they will dry ours when the time comes."

Gentle God, help us recognize the visible and invisible tears of those for whom we care today and every day.

Amen.

April 18

A week later his disciples were again in the house, and Thomas was with them. Although the doors were shut, Jesus came and stood among them and said, "Peace be with you." Then he said to Thomas, "Put your finger here and see my hands. Reach out your hand and put it in my side. Do not doubt but believe."

JOHN 20:26–27

Despite his doubt, Thomas was still a trusted disciple of Jesus at the end of this passage. None of us has perfect faith. All of us have doubts. The good news of the story of Thomas is that God still accepts and uses us—doubts and all—to better the kingdom.

Almighty God, while we may only have the faith of a mustard seed, use us fully for your kingdom.

Amen.

April 19

Then Peter, filled with the Holy Spirit, said to them,
"Rulers of the people and elders, if we are questioned
today because of a good deed done to someone who was
sick and are asked how this man has been healed, let it
be known to all of you, and to all people of Israel, that
this man is standing before you in good health by the
name of Jesus Christ of Nazareth, whom you crucified,
whom God raised from the dead."

ACTS 4:8–10

Before Peter speaks these words, he heals a crippled man. Healing was an integral part of the Apostle's ministry as it was in Jesus' ministry. Yet, the acts of healing were also seen as radical and disruptive to the religious authorities of the time. May we continue to find ways to practice radical hospitality toward our brothers and sisters today.

Healer God, may we be healing presences to all
the people around us today.

Amen.

April 20

*But know that the Lord has set apart the faithful
for himself; the Lord hears when I call to him.
When you are disturbed, do not sin; ponder it on
your beds and be silent.*

PSALM 4:3–4

When I read these verses I thought of the quote
by Thomas Jefferson, "When angry, count to
ten before you speak; if very angry, a hundred." It
is so easy to act on impulse, especially in those most
trying times of our lives, but we are reminded to
pause and let God inform our actions.

*Understanding God, you are with us always,
and for that, we thank you. Help us to be
better listeners for your voice in our lives.*

Amen.

April 21

"Very truly, I tell you, when you were younger,
you used to fasten your own belt and to go wherever
you wished. But when you grow old, you will
stretch out your hands, and someone else will fasten
a belt around you and take you where you do not wish
to go." (He said this to indicate the kind of
death by which he would glorify God.) After
this he said to him, "Follow me."

JOHN 21:18–19

Being a follower of Christ wasn't easy in the first centuries. The cost of discipleship was high, sometimes resulting in a follower's own death. Yet to stay true to Christ's teaching has always been the greatest challenge. Consider what it means to be a follower of Christ today.

Loving God, give us the strength to follow
wherever you lead us.

Amen.

April 22

Now the apostles and the believers who were in Judea heard that the Gentiles had also accepted the word of God. So when Peter went up to Jerusalem, the circumcised believers criticized him saying, "Why did you go to uncircumcised men and eat with them?"

ACTS 11:1–3

Are we much different today? Don't we tend to congregate with people who look like us, think like us and believe like us? As people of faith we are challenged to look more broadly at who our brothers and sisters are.

Gracious God, give me eyes that see the fullness of your creation and everyone in it.

Amen.

April 23

Be gracious to me, O Lord, for I am in distress;
my eye wastes away from grief, my soul and body
also. For my life is spent with sorrow, and my
years with sighing; my strength fails because of
my misery, and my bones waste away ... But I
trust in you, O Lord; I say, "You are my God."

PSALM 31:9–10, 14

This wonderful passage has the psalmist crying out the evidence that what affects our spirit also impacts our body. Our bodies and spirits are one. God calls us to care for all bodies and spirits, especially people who are left out of systems of care.

Merciful God, help us better sense
your presence at those times when our
spirits are wounded.

Amen.

April 24

*The Lord God has given me the tongue of a teacher,
that I may know how to sustain the weary with a
word. Morning by morning he wakens—wakens my
ear to listen as those who are taught.*

ISAIAH 50:4

The writer of this passage is identifying a gift
given to him by God. Have you identified a
gift given to you by God? Take a moment today to
consider your God-given gift. Thank God for that
gift, or pray that God will lead you to discover
your gift.

*Creator God, be with us this day as we
seek to do your will. Guide us so that we
can see your will for us.*

Amen.

April 25

*While they were eating, Jesus took a loaf of bread,
and after blessing it he broke it, gave it to the
disciples, and said, "Take, eat; this is my body."
Then he took a cup, and after giving thanks he gave
it to them, saying, "Drink from it, all of you; for this
is my blood of the covenant, which is poured out for
many for the forgiveness of sins."*

MATTHEW 26:26–28

Christians have many practices and traditions around Communion, the Lord's Supper, or the Eucharist, but a common thread of these traditions is intimately connecting with Jesus. Consider what the words "this is my body" say to you in your daily life.

*Ever-present God, help us better sense you
beside us in our daily walk with you.*

Amen.

April 26

Then Peter began to speak to them: "I truly understand that God shows no partiality, but in every nation anyone who fears him and does what is right is acceptable to him. You know the message he sent to the people of Israel, preaching peace by Jesus Christ—he is Lord of all."

ACTS 10:34–36

We strive for lives that have a sense of meaning and purpose. Imagine the coherence the disciples felt through their work with Jesus. Now imagine how that life-giving meaning was upset when Jesus was killed as a common criminal. Today, consider those people, those connections, and those beliefs which bring the most meaning into your life.

Faithful God, for those people, those institutions, for all that brings rich, life-giving meaning into our lives, we thank you.

Amen.

April 27

"But I replied, 'By no means, Lord; for nothing profane or unclean has ever entered my mouth.' But a second time the voice answered from heaven, 'What God has made clean, you must not call profane.'"

ACTS 11:8–9

Reading Peter's account of his vision reminded me that in the creation narrative, God stamps a seal of approval at each stage calling each "good." God created us in all our diversity. As children of God, we are bound together as relatives of one another.

Almighty God, you created us in your image.
Help us remember that this and every day.

Amen.

April 28

When he saw the crowds, he had compassion for them, because they were harassed and helpless, like sheep without a shepherd.
MATTHEW 9:36

The word pastor is derived from the Latin word for shepherd. According to an online dictionary, pastor can be used for a Christian minister or a layperson having spiritual charge over people. In a sense, we are all called to "pastor" others.

Gracious God, sometimes our responsibility toward one another seems too great. Help us remember that you are always with us.

Amen.

April 29

*Beloved, we are God's children now; what we will
be has not yet been revealed. What we do know is
this: when he is revealed, we will be like him,
for we will see him as he is.*

1 JOHN 3:2

As much as any other idea in Scripture, our
relationship as brothers and sisters informs my
understanding of our responsibility toward one
another. I know I often fall short in this regard, but
that is why it is called a faith journey.

*Steadfast God, thank you for standing by us
even when we are prone to wander.*

Amen.

April 30

How does God's love abide in anyone who has the world's goods and sees a brother or sister in need and yet refuses help? Little children, let us love, not in word or speech, but in truth and action.

1 JOHN 3:17–18

O ur faith should change us, transform us, but faith should not just make us think better thoughts about one another. Our faith should make us act in ways which convey love toward one another.

Loving God, as we grapple with our faith, help us always to see our neighbors as children of God.

Amen.

May

Cooking in the Nutrition Kitchen at Wellness.

May 1

*Now the whole earth had one language and the
same words. And as they migrated from the east,
they came upon a plain in the land of Shinar and
settled there ... Then they said, "Come, let us
build ourselves a city, and a tower with its top in
the heavens, and let us make a name for
ourselves; otherwise we shall be scattered abroad
upon the face of the whole earth."*

GENESIS 11:1–2, 4

Sharing a common language does not guarantee
universal understanding. Language is so
nuanced that a word can take on different meanings
depending on the inflection in one's voice or the
body language used in its delivery. Engage in active
listening today so that you might best understand
what is being said.

*Almighty God, help us be better
listeners today. Help us understand
what is actually being said.*

Amen.

May 2

*And the LORD said, "Look they are one people, and
they have all one language; and this is only the
beginning of what they will do; nothing that they
propose to do will now be impossible for them.
Come, let us go down, and confuse their language
there, so that they will not understand one
another's speech." ... Therefore it was called Babel,
because there the LORD confused the language of
all the earth; and from there the LORD scattered
them abroad over the face of all the earth.*

GENESIS 11:6–7, 9

The people of Babel wanted to "make a name for
ourselves" (verse 4). This passage reminds us
that we should be mindful, as best we can, to God's
will and not our will. Today we pray to be better
listeners to God.

*Gracious God, help us hear your voice in all
the ways you choose to speak to us.*

Amen.

May 3

Then I heard the voice of the LORD saying, "Whom shall I send, and who will go for us?" And I said, "Here am I; send me!"

ISAIAH 6:8

When Jesus calls his disciples, the Bible reports that they essentially drop what they are doing and follow him. In practice, finding our own calling can be a difficult and lifelong task. Yet to be called, one must first have an attitude of listening.

Loving God, incline our ears to you. Give us an attitude of listening so that we might hear your voice.

Amen.

May 4

Then Jesus said to them, "These are my words that I spoke to you while I was still with you — that everything written about me in the law of Moses, the prophets, and the psalms must be fulfilled." Then he opened their minds to understand the scriptures.

<small>LUKE 24:44–45</small>

I believe God is still speaking to us, and I see the life of faith as an ongoing conversation with God. Our prayer today is that each of us will hear God's voice in our lives.

Loving God, help us to be better listeners so that we will know your will for us.

Amen.

May 5

O Lord, how manifold are your works! In wisdom you have made them all; the earth is full of your creatures ... When you send forth your spirit, they are created; and you renew the face of the ground. May the glory of the Lord endure forever; may the Lord rejoice in his works.

Psalm 104:24, 30–31

We are reminded of the intimate relationship in which we live with God. The Holy Spirit surrounds us and inhabits us. Our challenge, I think, is to keep this connection to God in mind throughout each day.

Life-giving God, help us be aware of your constant presence so that we will draw on your strength in all we do.

Amen.

May 6

So when they had come together, they asked him,
"Lord, is this the time when you will restore the
kingdom to Israel?" He replied, "It is not for
you to know the times or periods that the Father
has set by his own authority.

ACTS 1:6–7

At my church, we welcome "people of faith and people of doubt" to our communion table. This passage reminds us that living with questions about our faith is expected and accepted.

Steadfast God, thank you for remaining by our
side as we walk faithfully toward you.

Amen.

May 7

*So we have known and believe the love that God
has for us. God is love, and those who abide in love
abide in God, and God abides in them … There is
no fear in love, but perfect love casts out fear; for
fear has to do with punishment, and whoever fears
has not reached perfection in love.*

1 JOHN 4:16, 18

O ften when I am fearful, I find myself in a
situation where I feel the need to rely only on
me. As my focus continues turning inward for a
solution to the specific situation, I begin to shut God
off from participating in my response. Open yourself
to what God is doing in your life today.

*Almighty God, your willingness to be present
in our lives is constant. Help us adopt the
habit of turning to you for everything.*

Amen.

May 8

*Come to him, a living stone, though rejected
by mortals yet chosen and precious in God's
sight, and like living stones, let yourselves
be built into a spiritual house, to be a holy
priesthood, to offer spiritual sacrifices
acceptable to God through Jesus Christ.*

1 PETER 2:4–5

I am moved by Peter's metaphor of living stones.
Our work is laid on the foundation created by
those who have come before us, and we are building
the foundation for the generation to come. Peter
emphasizes our interdependence on one another.

*Gracious God, bless our faith work as we seek
to build a lasting witness to your love for us.*

Amen.

May 9

*All who believed were together and had all things in
common; they would sell their possessions and goods
and distribute the proceeds to all, as any had need.*

ACTS 2:44–45

The shepherd provides beautiful imagery of how
God interacts with us—protecting us, providing
for us, leading us. This Scripture from Acts reminds
us that we are called to shepherd one another. Take
a moment to think of someone who has shepherded
you, and thank God for that person.

*Gracious God, thank you for the many
shepherds in our lives. Make us more sensitive
to the needs of others so that we might be
better shepherds ourselves.*

Amen.

May 10

"All mine are yours, and yours are mine; and I have been glorified in them. And now I am no longer in the world, but they are in the world, and I am coming to you. Holy Father, protect them in your name that you have given me, so that they may be one, as we are one."

JOHN 17:10–11

I n the moments before his betrayal, this prayer shows us that Jesus's thoughts were turned toward those who had followed him and who would carry on his ministry. In subsequent verses of this prayer, Jesus even prays for us asking that we may be "brought to complete unity." This is a beautiful prayer with a beautiful thought for this day.

Eternal God, help us to know you better
so that we can be of the same mind
with one another.

Amen.

May 11

Then Stephen knelt down and cried out in a loud voice, "Lord, do not hold this sin against them." When he had said this, he died.

ACTS 7:60

I can't imagine the pain, fear, and humiliation of being stoned to death. What I also can't fathom is Stephen's ability to cry out during this horrible experience, "Forgive these men!" Ours is a faith of loving both enemies and neighbors. Stephen forgave his executioners just as Jesus had done. Today, consider for a minute the challenge of offering such radical forgiveness.

Gracious God, you call us to forgive not only when it is simple, but when it really costs us. Help us in our efforts to be more forgiving.

Amen.

May 12

This is my commandment, that you love one another
as I have loved you. No one has greater love than this,
to lay down one's life for one's friends.

JOHN 15:12–13

I t is so easy to say "Love your neighbor as
yourself," yet Jesus's love for us was a sacrificial
love. We are called to love one another as Jesus loves
us. Imagine for a moment today what kind of world
we would live in if everyone loved sacrificially.

Loving God, help us to love one
another as you love us.

Amen.

May 13

*Does not wisdom call, and does not understanding
raise her voice? On the heights, beside the way,
at the crossroads she takes her stand; beside the
gates in front of the town, at the entrance of
the portals she cries out: "To you, O people, I call,
and my cry is to all that live."*

PROVERBS 8:1–4

This passage encourages us to seek wisdom.
Pray for the knowledge, the understanding,
the perception and the good judgment that comes
with wisdom.

*Gracious God, help us be seekers of
wisdom this and every day.*

Amen.

May 14

One day, as we were going to the place of prayer, we met a slave-girl who had a spirit of divination and brought her owners a great deal of money by fortune-telling. While she followed Paul and us, she would cry out, "These men are slaves of the Most High God, who proclaim to you a way of salvation."

ACTS 16:16–17

While we long to hear the truth, we tend to expect that it will be presented in familiar and recognizable ways. This passage reminds us that God's truth can be revealed in unexpected and non-traditional ways.

Almighty God, give us ears to hear your truth in the multitude of ways it can be presented to us.

Amen.

May 15

*Sing to God, sing praises to his name; lift up a song
to him who rides upon the clouds—his name is the
LORD—be exultant before him. Father of orphans
and protector of widows is God in his holy
habitation. God gives the desolate a home to live in;
he leads out the prisoners to prosperity.*

PSALM 68:4–6

God: parent of the parentless, shelter-giver to the
shelter-less. God works in mysterious ways,
but God also works through us. I think of us as God's
hands and feet on earth, caring as best we can for
one another, especially for those least among us.

*Protector God, help us as we strive to make
your world gentler for all your children.*

Amen.

May 16

The voice of the LORD is powerful; the voice of the LORD is full of majesty. The voice of the LORD breaks the cedars; the LORD breaks the cedars of Lebanon.

PSALM 29:4–5

Cedars of Lebanon are trees towering to 120 feet with diameters reaching nine feet. This resilient wood had many uses in biblical times providing wood for ships as well as many temples (and much more recently rail road ties!). The resin of this tree was used to help mummify the dead, and the fragrant wood was often used as part of burnt offerings. The psalmist is placing God's strength above the strongest and most significant natural material known to the people of the time.

Almighty God, we pray this day that you break any chains that are binding us so that we can live fully engaged as your children.

Amen.

May 17

*In the year that King Uzziah died, I saw the Lord
sitting on a throne high and lofty; and the hem of his
robe filled the temple ... And I said, "Woe is me! I
am lost, for I am a man of unclean lips, and I live
among people of unclean lips; yet my eyes have seen
the King, the LORD of hosts!"*

ISAIAH 6:1, 5

A counselor once defined depression for me as
"hatred turned inward." When we look at
ourselves through our own distorted lens, the sight
is not always pretty. Colossians 3:12 says that we
are "God's chosen ones, holy and dearly loved,"
and today's passage challenges us to look at
ourselves through God's lens and not ours.

*Gracious God, we thank you this day for your
faith in and love for us.*

Amen.

May 18

In the last days it will be, God declares, that I will pour out my Spirit upon all flesh, and your sons and your daughters shall prophesy, and your young men shall see visions, and your old men shall dream dreams.

ACTS 2:17

In the benediction used at my church each Sunday, the pastor includes the line, "and the Holy Spirit, our strength, be with each of us." We are reminded that through God all things are possible—that even our visions and dreams might be your gentle nudgings.

Almighty God, you pour your Spirit out for us. May we use the strength and vision it gives us to build your kingdom.

Amen.

May 19

"I have said these things to you while I am still with you. But the Advocate, the Holy Spirit, whom the Father will send in my name, will teach you everything, and remind you of all that I have said to you. Peace I leave with you; my peace I give to you. I do not give to you as the world gives. Do not let your hearts be troubled, and do not let them be afraid."

JOHN 14:25–27

I find these words comforting because they confirm that our journey of faith is a process. We are offered the peace of Christ even when our knowledge might be incomplete.

Almighty God, may we always be seekers of your truth. Come, Holy Spirit, come.

Amen.

May 20

As the Father has loved me, so I have
loved you; abide in my love.
JOHN 15:9

Abide is such a wonderful word in this verse.
Abide can mean stand—stand in my love.
Abide can also mean rest—rest in my love.

Protector God, earthly love is often fleeting,
but your love for us is steadfast.
Thank you.

Amen.

May 21

*The LORD is my shepherd, I shall not want. He
makes me lie down in green pastures; he leads me
beside still waters; he restores my soul. He leads
me in right paths for his name's sake.*

PSALM 23:1–3

God's presence in our lives is restorative. I
imagine green pastures as places where rest is
possible or sustenance is taken in, and I see still
waters as places of calm. Close your eyes and picture
such a place. Now thank God for leading you there.

*Caring God, lead us in right paths so that our
work today furthers your kingdom.*

Amen.

May 22

*The wind blows where it chooses, and you hear
the sound of it, but you do not know where it
comes from or where it goes. So it is
with everyone who is born of the Spirit.*

JOHN 3:8

Years ago I learned the concept of the priesthood of all believers—the idea that all of us are ministers. The day I first learned about it has stuck with me for years and in retrospect, this was a Pentecost moment for me. Think for a moment today about a Pentecost moment in your life, and thank God for that revelation.

*Steadfast God, thank you for those times when
we can see and hear you more clearly.*

Amen.

May 23

While Peter was still speaking, the Holy Spirit fell upon all who heard the word. The circumcised believers who had come with Peter were astounded that the gift of the Holy Spirit had been poured out even on the Gentiles, for they heard them speaking in tongues and extolling God.

ACTS 10:44–46

As the disciples picked up Jesus's ministry they, like Jesus, surprised followers and religious leaders who witnessed events such as the one in today's passage. Remember that in God's perfect vision, people viewed as outcasts by their community or by social norms are often the very people called upon.

All knowing God, we want people to see your love reflected in our faces. May we see your love in theirs, too.

Amen.

May 24

I am the vine, you are the branches. Those who abide in me and I in them bear much fruit, because apart from me you can do nothing.

JOHN 15:5

Vines are strong, supportive plants that are not easily broken. When grown on arbors, vines also provide shelter. From birds' nests to pollen for bees, vines can be life-giving and sustaining. Strong, supportive, sheltering, life-sustaining. These are wonderful images of Jesus, too.

Loving God, you provide shelter from life's storms. You give us strength and life. Keep us mindful of these wonderful blessings.

Amen.

May 25

While she followed Paul and us she would cry out,
"These men are slaves of the Most High God, who
proclaim to you a way of salvation." She kept
doing this for many days. But Paul, very much
annoyed, turned and said to the spirit, "I order
you in the name of Jesus Christ to come out of
her." And it came out that very hour.

ACTS 16:17–19

I find it easy to forget that apostle Paul was merely human, so I treasure such passages as this one. The girl was speaking the truth, but she was saying it over and over again. Like many of us placed in a similar situation, Paul became very annoyed by her incessant talking, and he lost his patience and commanded the truth-speaking spirit to leave her.

Gracious God, grant us an extra
measure of patience today so that we
better serve those we meet.

Amen.

May 26

As she was going to bring the drink of water, Elijah
called to her and said, "Bring me a morsel of bread in
your hand." But she said, "As the LORD your God
lives, I have nothing baked, only a handful of meal in a
jar, and a little oil in a jug; I am now gathering a
couple of sticks, so that I may go home and prepare it
for myself and my son, that we may eat it, and die."

1 KINGS 17:11–12

We run into a number of people throughout the course of a day. Some, like the widow Elijah meets, may have lost all hope. My prayer today is that we will be able to discern those among us who are like the widow, so we can be most helpful to them.

Gracious God, help us be instillers of hope for
all those we meet today.

Amen.

May 27

Now who will harm you if you are eager to do what is good? But even if you do suffer for doing what is right, you are blessed. Do not fear what they fear, and do not be intimidated, but in your hearts sanctify Christ as Lord. Always be ready to make your defense to anyone who demands from you an accounting for the hope that is in you; yet do it with gentleness and reverence.

1 PETER 3:13–16

I can't imagine the difficulty of being a Christian in the first and second centuries. In a time of persecution, this advice from Peter held significant meaning for its readers. Paraphrased this might read, 'Be prepared to defend your beliefs, but do so with gentleness and with reverence.' This Scripture reminds us that we should consider ourselves representatives of God at all times.

Gracious God, help us remember you are with us always.

Amen.

May 28

"You will receive power when the Holy Spirit has come upon you; and you will be my witnesses in Jerusalem, in all Judea and Samaria, and to the ends of the earth." When he had said this, as they were watching, he was lifted up, and a cloud took him out of their sight.

ACTS 1:8–9

We often say that Jesus instructed his disciples to preach, teach, and heal. In this Scripture, we see how extensive their ministry was. We are striving to bring our message of hope and healing to the ends of the earth through our participation in local, regional, and national conferences, through our magazine *Church Health Reader*, and of course through the individual lives we touch here daily.

Almighty God, thank you for the many blessings you have bestowed upon the Church Health Center.

Amen.

May 29

"No, this is what was spoken through the prophet Joel: 'In the last days it will be, God declares, that I will pour out my Spirit upon all flesh, and your sons and your daughters shall prophesy, and your young men shall see visions, and your old men shall dream dreams. Even upon my slaves, both men and women, in those days I will pour out my Spirit; and they shall prophesy.'"

ACTS 2:16–18

Rev. Dr. Scott Morris once said, "The Church Health Center is a testament to what can be done when everyone does their part." Working together as the Spirit leads us individually and communally, we have changed thousands of lives since first opening in 1987.

Almighty God, for all your wonderful works, we thank you. Continue to use us so that we can realize your kingdom on earth.

Amen.

May 30

"I will not leave you orphaned; I am coming to you. In a little while the world will no longer see me, but you will see me; because I live, you also will live. On that day you will know that I am in my Father, and you in me, and I in you."

JOHN 14:18–20

I think the way we interact with people can help them sense God's presence in their lives. Today, embrace your role as a reflector of God's love back toward the people you meet.

Ever-present God, be with us as we interact with your children. May our actions help them see you more clearly.

Amen.

May 31

Happy are those who do not follow the advice of the
wicked, or take the path that sinners tread, or sit in the
seat of the scoffers; but their delight is in the law of the
LORD, and on his law they meditate day and night.
They are like trees planted by streams of water, which
yield their fruit in its season, and their leaves do not
wither. In all they do, they prosper.
PSALM 1:1–3

Sickness is one way people can experience drought in their lives. We should see our role as helping people develop deeper roots so they can withstand the droughts in life better. Our task is made easier if we can help them realize that there is a community of faith surrounding them so that they are never alone.

Gracious God, help us to be better
representatives of your love here on earth.

Amen.

June

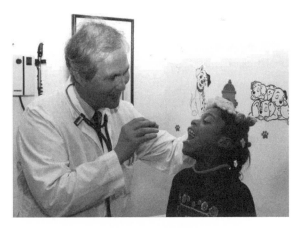

Dr. Scott Morris examines a young patient in the Clinic.

June 1

So Naaman came with his horses and chariots, and halted at the entrance of Elisha's house. Elisha sent a messenger to him, saying, "Go, wash in the Jordan seven times, and your flesh shall be restored and you shall be clean." But Naaman became angry and went away, saying, "… Are not Abana and Pharpar, the rivers of Damascus, better than all the rivers of Israel? Could I not wash in them, and be clean?" He turned and went away in a rage.

2 KINGS 5:9–12

One problem with the Internet is that we often think a simple search gives us the whole picture. Naaman didn't think the prescription offered by Elisha was adequate because of his preconceived notions. Consider how you might not be seeing an answer that is right in front of you.

God of all understanding, give us discerning minds to find the right path.

Amen.

June 2

*Happy are those whose transgression is forgiven,
whose sin is covered. Happy are those to whom the
LORD imputes no iniquity, and in whose spirit there is
no deceit…Many are the torments of the wicked, but
steadfast love surrounds those who trust in the LORD.*

PSALM 32:1–2, 10

We find ourselves pulling away from God sometimes. We might use power over someone in a way that hurts them. We are reminded in this passage that we worship a forgiving God who offers us steadfast love.

*Steadfast God, bless our efforts this day so
that they will reflect your will, and forgive
us if we fall short of the mark.*

Amen.

June 3

When the wife of Uriah heard that her husband was dead, she made lamentation for him. When the mourning was over, David sent and brought her to his house, and she became his wife, and bore him a son. But the thing David had done displeased the LORD and the LORD sent Nathan to David.

2 SAMUEL 11:26–12:1

Like King David, all of us have power over someone else. That power can be used in ways which build that person up, but we are reminded in this Scripture that power can be used to hurt, even to destroy, that person.

Loving God, help us treat one another as we would want to be treated.

Amen.

June 4

And I was still unknown by sight to the churches of Judea that are in Christ; they only heard it said, "The one who formerly was persecuting us is now proclaiming the faith he once tried to destroy." And they glorified God because of me.

<small>GALATIANS 1:22–24</small>

Paul's life is such a wonderful story of God's redemptive power. If a great persecutor of Christianity can become the person who provides such profound theological understanding, imagine how that redemptive power can work in each of us.

Steadfast and understanding God, turn our shortcomings into strengths that can be utilized to better your kingdom.

Amen.

June 5

*And just as Moses lifted up the serpent in the
wilderness, so must the Son of Man be lifted up, that
whoever believes in him may have eternal life.*

JOHN 3:14–15

The image of the serpent Moses created and held
aloft didn't keep the serpents from biting the
Israelites, but it kept the bitten Israelites from dying.
Similarly, Jesus' promise of eternal life does not
keep hardship from impacting us along the way,
but it does keep us from giving in to despair.

*Protector God, regardless of the
difficulties along our life's path, we
thank you for staying by our side.*

Amen.

June 6

*He said, "Go out and stand on the mountain before
the Lord, for the Lord is about to pass by." Now
there was a great wind, so strong that it was
splitting mountains and breaking rocks in pieces
before the Lord, but the Lord was not in the wind;
and after the wind, an earthquake, but the Lord was
not in the earthquake; and after the earthquake a fire,
but the Lord was not in the fire; and after the fire a
sound of sheer silence.*

1 Kings 19:11–12

On a mountain before the Lord, the prophet
Elijah found God in the "sheer silence." Take
a break from the tumult of your day. Listen for God
in the silence and calm.

*Gracious God, speak to us so that we will
know your will for us.*

Amen.

June 7

And on the seventh day God finished the work that he had done, and he rested on the seventh day from all the work that he had done. So God blessed the seventh day and hallowed it, because on it God rested from all the work that he had done in creation.

GENESIS 2:2–3

Like God, all of us need time to rest and recharge. Kingdom-building, peacemaking, justice-creating—there is much to be done, but it needs to be done over the long haul. Work hard, but take time to care for yourself.

Gracious God, help us order our lives so that rest and Sabbath-keeping are part of our service to you.

Amen.

June 8

There is no longer Jew or Greek, there is no longer slave or free, there is no longer male and female; for all of you are one in Christ Jesus.

GALATIANS 3:28

So many things can divide us—race, language, class. This passage asks us to focus on that which can join us—our practice of faith, our thirst for justice, and our love of God.

Almighty God, help us see your face in those we see today, and may they see your face in ours.

Amen.

June 9

*For just as the body is one and has many
members, and all the members of the body,
though many, are one body, so it is with Christ.*

1 CORINTHIANS 12:12

This passage confirms that each of us is both precious to God and vital to the building of God's kingdom. Whether you work at the Church Health Center, an insurance agency, a factory, a home—regardless of your actual job description, you are an agent of hope and healing and vital to God's kingdom.

*Loving God, help us embrace our gifts so
that we may be the kingdom-builders
you would have us be.*

Amen.

June 10

The wicked shall depart to Sheol, all the nations that forget God. For the needy shall not always be forgotten, nor the hope of the poor perish forever. Rise up, O Lord! Do not let mortals prevail; let the nations be judged before you.

PSALM 9:17–19

God works through us individually, but this Scripture reminds us that God works through us collectively as communities of believers. Many of us are doing our part to bring a measure of hope to the least among us with a powerful message from God: you are not forgotten.

Gracious God, bless our efforts to bring hope and healing to all we see this and every day.

Amen.

June 11

Now when the LORD was about to take Elijah up to heaven by a whirlwind, Elijah and Elisha were on their way from Gilgal. Elijah said to Elisha, "Stay here; for the LORD has sent me as far as Bethel." But Elisha said, "As the LORD lives, and as you yourself live, I will not leave you." So they went down to Bethel.

2 KINGS 2:1–2

Again in verse 6, Elisha is given a chance to stop traveling with Elijah, but he chooses to continue on the journey. Elisha's faithfulness to God and to Elijah runs deep. Consider today someone on whom you can depend always to be there for you, and give thanks to God for that person.

Almighty God, thank you for bringing loving, dependable, trustworthy people into our lives.

Amen.

June 12

*Discipline yourselves, keep alert. Like a roaring lion
your adversary the devil prowls around, looking for
someone to devour. Resist him, steadfast in your faith,
for you know your brothers and sisters in all the world
are undergoing the same kinds of suffering.*

1 PETER 5:8–9

"You're not the only one having a bad day!"
Have you ever said that to a friend, family
member or coworker? It is easy for us to
misunderstand each other, because we don't know
one another's full life story. It can help our
interactions with one another if we try to remember
that we have not "walked a mile" in our neighbor's
shoes. Let's be careful with each other.

*Loving God, help us to be better neighbors by
being more gentle with one another.*

Amen.

June 13

Humble yourselves therefore under the mighty hand of God, so that he may exalt you in due time. Cast all your anxiety on him, because he cares for you.

1 PETER 5:6–7

Life for all of us can have enormous highs, but it can also have excruciating lows. The beauty of a life of faith is that you open yourself to a relationship with a God who cares for you, with a God who is personally invested in you, with a God who hurts when you hurt.

Caring God, thank you for your steadfast presence in our lives.

Amen.

June 14

God did not make death, and he does not delight in the death of the living. For he created all things so that they might exist; the generative forces of the world are wholesome, and there is no destructive poison in them, and the dominion of Hades is not on earth. For righteousness is immortal.

WISDOM OF SOLOMON 1:13–15

Consider today how each of us as a part of God's creation is a generative force, a life-giving and life-enhancing presence, for one another.

Creator God, help us in our daily walk with you to be present in the lives of those around us in ways that are pleasing to you.

Amen.

June 15

*David said, "The LORD, who saved me from the paw of
the lion and from the paw of the bear, will save me
from the hand of this Philistine." So Saul said to
David, "Go, and may the LORD be with you!" Then
David took his staff in his hand, and chose five smooth
stones from the wadi, and put them in his shepherd's
bag, in the pouch; his sling was in his hand,
and he drew near the Philistine.*

1 SAMUEL 17:37, 40

D avid has put on all of Saul's weighty armor for
protection. Yet he takes the armor off because
he was not "used" to it. In this moment, David opts
to face Goliath wrapped only with the faith that
God would protect him.

*Gracious God, give us the faith of David so
that we are able to face all obstacles
remembering you are always by our side.*

Amen.

June 16

The LORD upholds all who are falling, and raises up all who are bowed down. The eyes of all look to you, and you give them their food in due season. You open your hand, satisfying the desire of every living thing. The LORD is just in all his ways, and kind in all his doings.

PSALM 145:14–17

I like the visual image of God holding my forearm and gently pressing a hand into my back supporting me so I can stand a bit taller. I hope that each of us has the opportunity today to prevent a fall or to help someone stand taller.

God of compassion, be with us in our walk with you today. Help us to be instruments of your kindness in all we do.

Amen.

June 17

But David said to the Philistine, "You come to me
with sword and spear and javelin; but I come to you in
the name of the LORD of hosts, the God of the armies of
Israel, whom you have defied." ... David put his hand
in his bag, took out a stone, slung it, and struck the
Philistine on his forehead; the stone sank into his
forehead, and he fell face down on the ground.

1 SAMUEL 17:45, 49

Consider for a moment a giant in your world,
something ominous looming ahead of you. An
interview, an exam, a presentation, or maybe a
person. David faced Goliath, the giant Philistine,
with a few stones, a slingshot and a deep, abiding
faith in God.

Almighty God, help us face the giants in our
lives with the assurance of David.

Amen.

June 18

Do not put your trust in princes, in mortals, in whom
there is no help. When their breath departs, they
return to earth; on that very day, their plans perish.
Happy are those whose help is the God of Jacob,
whose hope is in the LORD their God.

PSALM 146:3–5

We live with so many distractions—debt, loneliness, illness, the 24-hour news cycle. We are reminded by the passage today to focus on that which is eternal—God and God's love for us.

Almighty God, help us better understand
that which is eternal so that we can live
into your expectations of us.

Amen.

June 19

*Then all the tribes of Israel came to David at
Hebron, and said, "Look, we are your bone and
flesh ... The LORD said to you: It is you who shall
be shepherd of my people Israel, you who shall be
ruler over Israel." So all the elders of Israel came
to the king at Hebron; and King David made a
covenant with them at Hebron before the LORD,
and they anointed David king over Israel.*

2 SAMUEL 5:1–3

The people of Israel saw themselves as David's
flesh and bone. I like to think of us as God's
flesh and bone. May God speak to each of us so we
will know how best to respond to this awesome
responsibility.

*Gracious God, use our hands and
feet, our flesh and bone, in service to
you and your children.*

Amen.

June 20

The prayer of faith will save the sick, and the Lord will raise them up; and anyone who has committed sins will be forgiven. Therefore confess your sins to one another, and pray for one another, so that you may be healed. The prayer of the righteous is powerful and effective.

JAMES 5:15–16

In reading this passage today, I am struck that as people of faith we have to allow ourselves to be vulnerable to each other, to be able to confess our shortcomings to one another as well as to pray with one another.

Almighty God, give us the confidence to be vulnerable to one another.

Amen.

June 21

*Now there was a woman who had been suffering from
hemorrhages for twelve years. She had endured much
under many physicians, and had spent all that she had;
and she was no better, but rather grew worse. She had
heard about Jesus, and came up behind him in the
crowd and touched his cloak, for she said, "If I but
touch his clothes, I will be made well." Immediately
her hemorrhage stopped; and she felt in her body that
she was healed of her disease.*

MARK 5:25–29

This woman was healed of her physical ailment,
but bleeding for 12 years would have made her
ritually unclean for all that time. This would have
separated her from her community of faith and from
her God. Jesus healed her, restoring her relationship
with God and her community.

*God of restoration, help remove those barriers
that keep us separated from you.*

Amen.

June 22

He also said, "With what can we compare the kingdom of God, or what parable will we use for it? It is like a mustard seed, which, when sown upon the ground, is the smallest of all the seeds on earth; yet when it is sown it grows up to become the greatest of all shrubs, and puts forth large branches, so that the birds of the air can make nests in its shade."

MARK 4:30–32

With these words, Jesus challenges us to consider this question: from where does our hope come? When our faith is only that of a mustard seed, God can still do extraordinary things through us.

Loving God, our faith in you waxes and wanes, but you are steadfast in your love for us. Thank you for using us all those times we are less than 100 percent.

Amen.

June 23

*So we are always confident; even though we know that
while we are at home in the body we are away from the
Lord—for we walk by faith, not by sight. Yes, we do
have confidence, and we would rather be away from the
body and at home with the Lord.*

2 CORINTHIANS 5:6–8

Usually when we speak of having confidence,
we are referring to something that we have
seen. "I have performed the experiments, and the
data has provided me with confidence in the
conclusion." "I interviewed the job candidate, and
I am confident of her qualifications for the job." In
contrast, this passage reminds us that God asks us
to live confidently trusting God and to walk by faith,
not by sight.

*God of mystery, strengthen our faith so that
our life-walk can be made with confidence.*

Amen.

June 24

For freedom Christ has set us free. Stand firm, therefore, and do not submit again to a yoke of slavery ... For you were called to freedom, brothers and sisters; only do not use your freedom as an opportunity for self-indulgence, but through love become slaves to one another. For the whole law is summed up in a single commandment, "You shall love your neighbor as yourself."

GALATIANS 5:1, 13–14

Paul reminds us that we are called to a radical love for one another, to become as brothers and sisters to one another. As you meet people today, consider how this passage informs your interaction with them.

Understanding God, you call us to a deeper level of love for one another. Continue to nudge us toward your will.

Amen.

June 25

Then they arrived at the country of the Gerasenes,
which is opposite Galilee. As Jesus stepped out on
land, a man of the city who had demons met him. For a
long time he had worn no clothes, and he did not live
in a house but in the tombs.

Luke 8:26–27

Imagine this scene for a moment: a naked, ritually unclean man approached Jesus shouting, as the Scripture says in the next verse, at the top of his voice. While most of us would have crossed to the other side of the street quickly, Jesus confronted the demons and healed this poor man.

Understanding God, help us keep our
perspective this and every day, especially when
we are confronted by some of your more
troubled children.

Amen.

June 26

The Lord listened to the voice of Elijah; the life of the child came into him again, and he revived. Elijah took the child, brought him down from the upper chamber into the house, and gave him to his mother; then Elijah said, "See, your son is alive." So the woman said to Elijah, "Now I know that you are a man of God, and that the word of the Lord in your mouth is truth."

1 KINGS 17:22–24

It took a miracle for the woman to believe the words of Elijah. Most of us won't have the privilege of delivering a miracle to someone, so we are left with people believing our words based on other cues. May our sincerity and truth be understood by those who meet us.

*Loving God, may people see your face in ours,
and may we see your face in theirs.*

Amen.

June 27

*Whoever welcomes you welcomes me, and whoever
welcomes me welcomes the one who sent me. Whoever
welcomes a prophet in the name of a prophet will
receive a prophet's reward; and whoever welcomes a
righteous person in the name of a righteous person will
receive the reward of the righteous; and whoever gives
even a cup of cold water to one of these little ones
in the name of a disciple—truly I tell you,
none of these will lose their reward.*

MATTHEW 10:40–42

A commentary on these verses described "these little ones" as "ordinary" disciples. That sounds like most of us, doesn't it? We live out our faith in many ways. This scripture reminds us that one way is by simply practicing hospitality.

*Gracious God, thank you for welcoming us.
Help us to be better at welcoming others.*

Amen.

June 28

O LORD, our Sovereign, how majestic is your name in all the earth! When I look at your heavens, the work of your fingers, the moon and the stars you have established; what are human beings that you are mindful of them, mortals that you care for them? Yet you have made them a little lower than God, and crowned them with glory and honor. You have given them dominion over the works of your hands.

PSALM 8:1, 3–6

I often use the phrase kingdom-builders to describe our role as God's hands and feet on earth, but we are also kingdom-tenders. Think of one more thing you could do to be a better caretaker of God's creation, then ask for God's help in making it happen.

Trusting God, help us as we strive to be better stewards of your creation which you have entrusted to us.

Amen.

June 29

Then one of the leaders of the synagogue named
Jairus came and, when he saw Jesus, fell at his
feet and begged him repeatedly, "My little
daughter is at the point of death. Come and lay
your hands on her, so that she may be made well,
and live." So he went with him. And a large
crowd followed him and pressed in on him.

MARK 5:22–24

What moves me about this passage is the lack
of discussion between Jesus and Jairus. Jairus
pleads with Jesus to make his daughter well, and
verse 24 simply states, "So Jesus went with him."
As you consider this passage today, think about
how it directs us in our responsibility toward
children and their health and welfare.

Creator God, keep us mindful of the needs
of the children in our lives.

Amen.

June 30

For God so loved the world that he gave his only Son,
so that everyone who believes in him may not perish
but may have eternal life.

JOHN 3:16

God loves us sacrificially, and in doing so, God challenges us to love one another in a similar fashion. It is easy to say, "I love you," but this popular passage calls us, as people of faith, to a depth of love for one another that is usually reserved for blood relatives.

Understanding God, open our hearts to all our
brothers and sisters, and help us to understand
the depth of love for one another you expect.

Amen.

July

Farmer's Market outside Wellness.

July 1

The apostles gathered around Jesus, and told him all that they had done and taught. He said to them, "Come away to a deserted place all by yourselves and rest a while." For many were coming and going, and they had no leisure even to eat.

MARK 6:30–31

While we are called to care for one another, this passage clearly reminds us that we are also to care for ourselves. We can't serve others or serve God effectively if we are hungry or tired. Are you caring for yourself as much as you are caring for others?

Almighty God, thank you for reminding us that you want us to care for ourselves as well as our brothers and sisters.

Amen.

July 2

When David had finished offering the burnt-offerings and the offerings of well-being, he blessed the people in the name of the LORD of hosts, and distributed food among all the people, the whole multitude of Israel, both men and women, to each a cake of bread, a portion of meat, and a cake of raisins. Then all the people went back to their homes.

2 SAMUEL 6:18–19

When David brought the ark of God to Jerusalem, they celebrated with the distribution of food. We continue this ancient practice when we gather for meals, be it a Wednesday-night supper, a soup kitchen, or a prayer breakfast. Today, make a commitment to bring a heart-healthy or diabetic-friendly dish as your contribution to your next church gathering.

Loving God, thank you for the times that we gather to share a meal together in your name.

Amen.

July 3

When Jesus saw the crowd, he had compassion for them, because they were harassed and helpless, like sheep without a shepherd.

MATTHEW 9:36

A shepherd must be concerned about all the aspects of the flock including nutrition, hydration, and rest. God's concern for us as a shepherd includes these same issues in addition to concern about our spirits.

Loving God, lead us where you would have us go and help us be spiritual and physical sustenance to our brothers and sisters.

Amen.

July 4

Come to me, all you that are weary and are carrying heavy burdens, and I will give you rest. Take my yoke upon you, and learn from me; for I am gentle and humble in heart, and you will find rest for your souls. For my yoke is easy, and my burden is light.

MATTHEW 11:28–30

Today, Jesus calls us to take on the "yoke" of discipleship and find our spiritual rest. Reflect on how you can find peace in your work and hope in your struggles.

Gracious God, you are more patient with us than we are with ourselves. You love us more than we love ourselves. Help us see ourselves more as you see us.

Amen.

July 5

Some wandered in desert wastes, finding no way to an inhabited town; hungry and thirsty, their soul fainted within them ... Let them thank the LORD for his steadfast love, for his wonderful works to humankind. For he satisfies the thirsty, and the hungry he fills with good things.

PSALM 107:4–5, 8–9

This passage speaks of soul care. It reminds us that while taking care of physical needs, our spiritual needs are also buoyed up. Faith and health are intricately joined within each of us.

Gracious God, give us this day our daily bread, and help our spirits soar.

Amen.

July 6

"Give us each day our daily bread. And forgive us our sins, for we ourselves forgive everyone indebted to us. And do not bring us to the time of trial."

LUKE 11:3–4

We do not ask for a banquet, but rather we pray to God to provide for our basic biological needs. We pray to remain healthy in spirit as we face our day-to-day temptations. The prayer Jesus would have us pray asks God to provide for both our body and our spirit.

Faithful God, provide us with the strength to walk in your light every day.

Amen.

July 7

*I have not lived in a house since the day I brought up
the people of Israel from Egypt to this day, but I have
been moving about in a tent and a tabernacle.*

2 SAMUEL 7:6

God is speaking to the prophet Nathan in this
passage. God has been moving with the
Israelites since they came out of Egypt. Consider
how God is moving in your life today.

*Gracious God, help us feel your presence with
us today, and help us better share that
presence with others.*

Amen.

July 8

*If God is for us, who is against us? ... For I am
convinced that neither death, nor life, nor angels, nor
rulers, nor things present, nor things to come, nor
powers, nor height nor depth, nor anything else in all
creation, will be able to separate us from the love of
God in Christ Jesus our Lord.*

ROMANS 8: 31, 38–39

Despite feelings of loneliness and isolation, despite our fears, despite forces of nature and forces of human creation, God is our steadfast, ever-present ally.

*Gracious God, keep us mindful that you are
always by our side, and help us help those who
come before us today to feel your presence, too.*

Amen.

July 9

I know a person in Christ who fourteen years ago was caught up to the third heaven—whether in the body or out of the body I do not know; God knows.

2 CORINTHIANS 12:2

While my faith journey has answered some of my questions, it has also raised many questions. As part of my journey, I have had to grow comfortable with the phrase in today's verse, "I do not know; God knows." I pray that in time, God's time, my questions will be answered.

Loving God, we see in a mirror dimly today, and we look forward to that day when we see face to face.

Amen.

July 10

So if you have been raised with Christ, seek the things that are above, where Christ is, seated at the right hand of God. Set your minds on things that are above, not on things that are on earth, for you have died, and your life is hidden with Christ in God.

Colossians 3:1–3

Paul speaks of our faith as transforming our lives, and that as people of faith we have a different set of priorities. Consider how your faith has changed you and examine those parts of your life where you are resisting this change.

Steadfast God, bless our journey toward a fuller understanding of your will for us.

Amen.

July 11

He was praying in a certain place, and after he had finished, one of his disciples said to him, "LORD, teach us to pray, as John taught his disciples." He said to them, "When you pray, say: Father, hallowed be your name. Your kingdom come."

LUKE 11:1–2

Jesus asks that we first acknowledge the parental nature of God's love for us. Our relationship to God is as intimate as that of a parent—"Our Father, our Parent, who art in heaven."

Gracious God, who loves us as the perfect parent, use us as instruments of your will as we build your kingdom here on earth.

Amen.

July 12

"So I say to you, Ask, and it will be given you; search, and you will find; knock, and the door will be opened for you. For everyone who asks receives, and everyone who searches finds, and for everyone who knocks, the door will be opened."

LUKE 11:9–10

After teaching the disciples to pray, Jesus assures the disciples that the journey of faith is a worthwhile one. God listens. God answers.

Almighty God, thank you for your steadfast presence in our lives and for the gentle nudges when we veer off course.

Amen.

July 13

Steadfast love and faithfulness will meet;
righteousness and peace will kiss each other.
Faithfulness will spring up from the ground, and
righteousness will look down from the sky.

Psalm 85:10–11

We put our faith into action each day. We can all create a grassroots movement of neighborly love. May God bless our actions today and every day.

Loving God, while we may stumble along
the way, help us as we faithfully walk
toward your will.

Amen.

July 14

Now when Jesus heard this, he withdrew from there in a boat to a deserted place by himself. But when the crowds heard it, they followed him on foot from the towns. When he went ashore, he saw a great crowd; and he had compassion for them and cured their sick.

MATTHEW 14:13–14

This is the start of Matthew's account of the miracle of feeding the 5,000. In the verses prior to this one, Jesus has just learned that his friend, John the Baptist, has been killed, so Jesus was trying to get away, likely to grieve, but the crowds followed him. Duty often gets in the way in our own lives, and I take comfort knowing that Jesus needed time to himself before coming back ashore.

Compassionate God, thank you for moments of solitude when we can grieve or heal or rest. Thank you for being with us, giving us strength to continue.

Amen.

July 15

*The Lord is gracious and merciful, slow to anger
and abounding in steadfast love. The Lord is good
to all, and his compassion is over all that he has
made ... The Lord upholds all who are falling, and
raises up all who are bowed down.*

<small>Psalm 145:8–9, 14</small>

I can't help but notice the language of healing
in the last verse. We can fall and be bowed
down in so many ways, both physically and
spiritually. God is there for us helping us toward
health and wholeness.

> *Gracious God of compassion, we give
> thanks to you for being by our side
> throughout our life journey.*
>
> *Amen.*

July 16

*Then Jesus said to them, "Very truly, I tell you, it was
not Moses who gave you the bread from heaven, but it
is my Father who gives you the true bread from
heaven. For the bread of God is that which comes down
from heaven and gives life to the world."*

JOHN 6:32–33

With God inside and around us, I believe we become some of that heavenly bread that God offers his children. My prayer is that we will provide spiritual sustenance, some of heaven's bread, to each person we meet today.

*Sustainer God, help us be ambassadors of your
love to those we meet today.*

Amen.

July 17

*Therefore because you trample on the poor and take
from them levies of grain, you have built houses of
hewn stone, but you shall not live in them; you have
planted vineyards, but you shall not drink their wine.*

Amos 5:11

This passage clearly reminds us that God cares
about the poor. But it is also clear that God cares
about both our attitudes and our actions toward
the poor.

*Loving God, may your Spirit inform
our thoughts and actions toward
others each and every day.*

Amen.

July 18

Give justice to the weak and the orphan;
maintain the right of the lowly and the destitute.
Rescue the weak and the needy; deliver them
from the hand of the wicked.

PSALM 82:3–4

In today's passage, the psalmist reminds us of our responsibility to one another, especially to those less fortunate than we are. Consider today how your daily activities make the world more just for everyone.

Gracious God, bless our efforts this and every
day to make the world a gentler place for all.

Amen.

July 19

*Other seeds fell on rocky ground, where they did
not have much soil, and they sprang up quickly,
since they had no depth of soil. But when the sun
rose, they were scorched; and since they had no
root, they withered away.*

Matthew 13:5–6

A re you ever frustrated by the person who takes
your sound advice and embraces it for a week
or two only to fall back into old patterns and habits?
Remember what Mother Teresa said, "The good you
do today will often be forgotten. Do good anyway."

*Patient God, work within those we
meet today so that our efforts might
take deep root in their lives.*

Amen.

July 20

Other seeds fell among good soil and brought forth grain, some a hundredfold, some sixty, some thirty.
MATTHEW 13:8

This is the conclusion of Jesus' parable of the sower. Be generous in your spreading of seeds, for some of your seeds will fall on rich, good soil. Reflecting on Mother Teresa again today, she said, "Give the best you have, and it will never be enough. Give your best anyway."

God of abundance, help us see the potential in each person we meet today, and help us never to lose faith in what we are doing to help.

Amen.

July 21

O LORD, who may abide in your tent? Who may
dwell on your holy hill? Those who walk blamelessly,
and do what is right, and speak the truth from their
heart; who do not slander with their tongue, and do
no evil to their friends, nor take up a reproach
against their neighbors.

PSALM 15:1–3

Each day is a struggle to dwell on God's holy hill,
and how we treat one another matters to God.
Speak truth from your heart today.

Gracious God, work within us so that we can
better see those around us as you see them.

Amen.

July 22

"Which of these three, do you think, was a neighbor to the man who fell into the hands of the robbers?" He said, "The one who showed him mercy." Jesus said to him, "Go and do likewise."

LUKE 10:36–37

The story of the Good Samaritan reminds us that being a neighbor is not always easy, yet it is what we are asked to do each day.

Steadfast and understanding God, thank you for your mercy toward us as we stumble forward trying to be the neighbors you want us to be.

Amen.

July 23

The earth is the Lord's and the all that is in it, the world, and those who live in it; for he has founded it on the seas, and established it on the rivers.

Psalm 24:1–2

Are we individuals or part of a community? Are we soloists or part of a choir? Are we free agents or team players? We are the Lord's, and therefore we can't escape the communal nature of our relationship to one another.

Almighty God, bless our efforts this and every day to build the kind of community, the kind of kingdom, you would have.

Amen.

July 24

*Do not lie to one another, seeing that you have
stripped off the old self with its practices and have
clothed yourselves with the new self, which is being
renewed in knowledge according to the image of its
creator. In that renewal there is no longer Greek and
Jew, circumcised and uncircumcised, barbarian,
Scythian, slave and free; but Christ is all and in all!*

COLOSSIANS 3:9–11

The waiting room of the Church Health Center's
clinic can be a snapshot of the world's religions.
Our job isn't to make our patients believe like us,
but we do strive to let each person served know
that they are a child of God, deserving of our
loving care.

*Everlasting God, help us live lives that always
speak to others of our faith in you.*

Amen.

July 25

*I hated all my toil in which I had toiled under
the sun, seeing that I must leave it to those
who come after me—and who knows whether
they will be wise or foolish? Yet they will be
master of all for which I toiled and used my
wisdom under the sun. This also is vanity.*

ECCLESIASTES 2:18–19

We don't serve God alone but in a web of
relationships that extends from those who
came before us to those who follow us. Part of our
faith journey is trusting that our successors will
listen for God's voice as we have.

*Almighty God, grant that our ears might hear
you speaking to us and that our hearts might
better understand your will.*

Amen.

July 26

*And the Lord said, "If I find at Sodom fifty righteous
in the city, I will forgive the whole place for their
sake." Abraham answered, "Let me take it upon myself
to speak to the Lord, I who am but dust and ashes.
Suppose five of the fifty righteous are lacking? Will
you destroy the whole city for lack of five? And he said,
"I will not destroy it if I find forty-five there."*

GENESIS 18:26–28

God and Abraham speak back and forth for a few
more verses. As we reflect on this passage, we
begin to appreciate anew how, through God, one
person can make a significant difference in the world.

*Almighty God, be with us in our individual
and collective efforts to better your creation.*

Amen.

July 27

"And the slaves of the householder came and said to him, 'Master, did you not sow good seed in your field? Where, then, did these weeds come from?' He answered, 'An enemy has done this.' The slaves said to him, 'Then do you want us to go and gather them?' But he replied, 'No, for in gathering the weeds you would uproot the wheat along with them.'"

MATTHEW 13:27–29

We sometimes forget how interdependent we are and how our actions can have unintended consequences. We worship a patient God who is slow to anger and gentle with each of us. God asks us to do the same for one another.

Wonderful God, help us in our journey to be the neighbors you want us to be.

Amen.

July 28

*Although you are sovereign in strength, you judge
with mildness, and with great forbearance you govern
us; for you have power to act whenever you choose.*

WISDOM OF SOLOMON 12:18

I love the image of God offered by this passage. Be
gentle and patient with one another, for that is
how God is with us.

*Almighty God, we can be very hard on
one another. Mold us into more gentle
and forgiving followers.*

Amen.

July 29

*Jacob was left alone; and a man wrestled
with him until daybreak.*

Genesis 32:24

Jacob wanted to be alone and feared for his life.
But through wrestling with a man, God's presence
became apparent. No matter how alone we might
feel or how much we might struggle, God remains
a steadfast presence in our lives.

*Eternal God, when we go through dark hours
in our lives, may we be especially mindful of
your constant presence.*

Amen.

July 30

*Be mindful of your mercy, O LORD, and of your
steadfast love, for they have been from of old. Do not
remember the sins of my youth or my transgressions;
according to your steadfast love remember me, for your
goodness' sake, O LORD!*

PSALM 25:6–7

All of us have a skeleton or two in our closet.
For some of us, the past can be a terrible burden
to overcome. In this passage, the Psalmist reminds
us of God's steadfast love for us that is able to
overcome any of our own transgressions.

*Loving God, we are imperfect people
who are bathed in your perfect love. Grant
that our chosen path is always one that is
moving toward you. Gently nudge us
back when we stray.*

Amen.

July 31

So then you are no longer strangers and aliens,
but you are citizens with the saints and also members
of the household of God, built upon the foundation
of the apostles and prophets, with Christ Jesus
himself as the cornerstone.

Ephesians 2:19–20

When you construct a house, the foundation matters most. In his letter to the Ephesians, Paul is telling them that they, the people of God, are building the house together on the solid foundations of the prophets and apostles.

Creator God, may each person we meet today
see your face reflecting back to them.

Amen.

August

Volunteers work on a mailing.

August 1

A good name is to be chosen rather than great riches, and a favor is better than silver or gold. The rich and the poor have this in common: the Lord is the maker of them all.

PROVERBS 22:1–2

We often talk about having a "good name" as a mark of our reputation. This passage reminds us that we are all brothers and sisters in God's eyes and that caring for one another is of paramount importance. Today, let the mercy you show others be a way you establish your "good name."

Gracious God, help us recognize each other as intricately connected through you.

Amen.

August 2

*"But when you are invited to a wedding banquet,
go and sit at the lowest place, so that when your
host comes, he may say to you, 'Friend, move up
higher'; then you will be honored in the presence of
all who sit at the table with you. For all who exalt
themselves will be humbled, and those who humble
themselves will be exalted."*

Luke 14:10–11

A wedding banquet in Christ's time could refer
to any number of feasts, including dinner at
the home of a Pharisee. Jesus uses this setting to
remind us that we are asked to keep our egos in
check and to keep ourselves in proper perspective.

*Loving God, help us see ourselves as
children sharing a common parentage.
May this perspective guide our actions
toward one another.*

Amen.

August 3

Let mutual love continue. Do not neglect to show
hospitality to strangers, for by doing that some have
entertained angels without knowing it. Remember
those who are in prison, as though you were in prison
with them; those who are being tortured, as though
you yourselves were being tortured.

HEBREWS 13:1–3

B e hospitable to all, including those you don't
know. Always consider the suffering of others
as though you were suffering in the same way.
Consider today a world in which each of us walks
a mile in the other's shoes.

Gracious God, help us better care for
our brothers and sisters who through
you are as related to us as the family
members of our birth.

Amen.

August 4

*What to me is the multitude of your sacrifices? says
the Lord; I have had enough of burnt-offerings of
rams and the fat of fed beasts; I do not delight in the
blood of bulls, or of lambs, or of goats … Wash
yourselves; make yourselves clean; remove the evil of
your doings from before my eyes; cease to do evil,
learn to do good; seek justice, rescue the oppressed,
defend the orphan, plead for the widow.*

Isaiah 1:11, 16–17

God, speaking to Isaiah, is telling him that he is
not interested in the actions of people offering
him sacrifices. What God wants are actions that
impact our neighbors—doing good, seeking justice,
helping those who struggle to help themselves.

*Loving God, help us as we try to come to the
aid of our neighbors this and every day.*

Amen.

August 5

Contribute to the needs of the saints; extend hospitality to strangers. Bless those who persecute you; bless and do not curse them. Rejoice with those who rejoice, weep with those who weep. If it is possible, so far as it depends on you, live peaceably with all.

ROMANS 12:13–15, 18

Paul's rules ask us to live empathetically and to act with compassion: be a genuine presence to all, including strangers, and do the best you can to live in peace with everyone.

God of understanding, living together as neighbors can be hard work. Stand beside us in our efforts to be the people you want us to be.

Amen.

August 6

For as in one body we have many members, and not all the members have the same function, so we, who are many, are one body in Christ, and individually we are members one of another.

ROMANS 12:4–5

I find Paul's "body of Christ" language helpful when considering the workplace. Each person has a different job description and set of responsibilities. But each is asked to do God's kingdom-work. This means all jobs are vital and important.

Ever-present God, be with us this and every day as we walk faithfully with you among your people.

Amen.

August 7

Be careful then how you live, not as unwise people but as wise, making the most of the time, because the days are evil. So do not be foolish, but understand what the will of the Lord is.

EPHESIANS 5:15–17

Live engaged! Develop a vision of what God wants you to do then live into that vision.

Loving God, grant us wisdom to discern your will and grant us the courage to live into that will.

Amen.

August 8

If you refrain from trampling the sabbath, from pursuing your own interests on my holy day; if you call the sabbath a delight and the holy day of the LORD honorable; if you honor it, not going your own ways, serving your own interests, or pursuing your own affairs; then you shall take delight in the LORD, and I will make you ride upon the heights of the earth.

ISAIAH 58:13–14

God rested on the seventh day and declared it holy. Each of us is asked to set aside one day each week to distance ourselves from our earthly concerns to rest in God's glory. Consider today the ways you both recognize and ignore the Sabbath in your own life.

Everlasting God, to you we give the glory. Help us trust you enough so that we can be better observers of the Sabbath in our own lives.

Amen.

August 9

Then Jesus called the crowd to him and said to them, "Listen and understand: it is not what goes into the mouth that defiles a person, but it is what comes out of the mouth that defiles."

MATTHEW 15:10–11

Have you ever said something to a friend or loved one that you wished you hadn't said? Have you used a tone that conveyed something you didn't intend? I don't always say the right thing, but I try to recognize when I am defiling myself or others with my words, and apologize.

Understanding God, our voices can be powerful instruments. Help us use them for peace.

Amen.

August 10

Religion that is pure and undefiled before God, the Father, is this: to care for orphans and widows in their distress, and to keep oneself unstained by the world.

JAMES 1:27

One synonym for pure is undiluted. I found that an interesting word for this passage since diluting often makes something weaker or less reactive. So, be strong and work to rise above the fray of this world, and care for those less fortunate.

Caring God, keep us mindful of people less fortunate than we are.

Amen.

August 11

*When the LORD saw that Moses had turned
aside to see, God called to him out of the bush,
"Moses, Moses!" And he said, "Here I am."
Then God said, "Come no closer! Remove the
sandals from your feet, for the place on which
you are standing is holy ground."*

EXODUS 3:4–5

I think we stand on holy ground throughout the
day. Each time we are with someone else, a fellow
child of God, we are on holy ground. Whether you
are with a family member or a person seeking
services from you, honor the time and God's
presence there.

*Loving God, help us recognize your presence
in those around us. Help us walk faithfully on
the holy ground surrounding your children.*

Amen.

August 12

Reuben said to them, "Shed no blood; throw Joseph into this pit here in the wilderness, but lay no hand on him"—that he might rescue him and out of their hand and restore him to his father. So when Joseph came to his brothers, they stripped him of his robe, the long robe with the sleeves that he wore; and they took him and threw him into a pit. The pit was empty; there was no water in it.

GENESIS 37:22–24

The robe was so much a part of Joseph's self image that he wore it in front of his brothers despite knowing their feelings about it. I wonder how many people we see today will, in some way, feel stripped or robbed of that very thing that gives—or gave—meaning to their lives.

Merciful God, we will meet people today with hidden stories of pain and suffering. Give us gentle spirits to provide comfort for them.

Amen.

August 13

*But take care and watch yourselves closely, so as
to neither to forget the things that your eyes
have seen nor to let them slip from your mind all
the days of your life; make them known to your
children and your children's children.*

DEUTERONOMY 4:9

We learn from our life experiences. Sometimes those lessons are found in times of laughter, but others are found in times of great anguish. This scripture reminds us that we owe it to others, especially our families, to share those life lessons.

*Loving God, may we grow in our
wisdom, and may others benefit from
our passing on of that wisdom.*

Amen.

August 14

"But among you there are some who do not believe …"
And he said, "For this reason I have told you that no
one can come to me unless it is granted by the Father."
Because of this many of his disciples turned back and
no longer went about with him. So Jesus asked the
twelve, "Do you also wish to go away?"

JOHN 6:64–67

Turning points in life. That is what this passage
made me think about today. Those times in life
we come to a fork in the road and we can't take both
routes. How can we evaluate each route through
the lens of our faith and choose accordingly?

Gracious God, help us remember you are our
ever-present guide on the road of life.

Amen.

August 15

Do not be conformed to this world, but be transformed by the renewing of your minds, so that you may discern what is the will of God—what is good and acceptable and perfect.

ROMANS 12:2

I am reminded of salmon and their quest to swim upstream against seemingly impossible odds. It is so easy to go with the flow, and yet our faith calls us to be different—to be changed by it.

God, give us strength each day to meet the challenges we face during our walk of faith with you.

Amen.

August 16

Come, O children, listen to me; I will teach you the fear of the LORD. Which of you desires life, and covets many days to enjoy good? Keep your tongue from evil, and your lips from speaking deceit. Depart from evil, and do good; seek peace, and pursue it.

PSALM 34:11–14

Speak the truth. Do good. Seek and pursue peace.

*Understanding God, we want to be
truthful peacemakers in your world, but
we often fall short of this mark. Thank you
for loving us anyway.*

Amen.

August 17

Therefore take up the whole armor of God, so that you may be able to withstand on that evil day, and having done everything, to stand firm.

<small>EPHESIANS 6:13</small>

Paul admonishes us to put on truth, righteousness, peace, faith, salvation, and the Spirit. He then tells us to pray.

Almighty God, clothe us in your armor so that we will be the people you want us to be.

Amen.

August 18

Now if you are unwilling to serve the LORD, choose this day whom you will serve ... but as for me and my household, we will serve the LORD.

JOSHUA 24:15

Joshua is leading by example in this familiar passage: "It is your choice, but I am going to serve the Lord." This passage reminds me that each of us is an example for those around us. My prayer is that God's light will shine through us this day.

Loving God, help us reflect your will in all we do today and every day.

Amen.

August 19

*Then David slept with his ancestors, and was buried
in the city of David. The time that David reigned over
Israel was forty years; he reigned seven years in
Hebron and thirty-three years in Jerusalem. So
Solomon sat on the throne of his father David; and his
kingdom was firmly established.*

1 KINGS 2:10–12

Just prior to his death, David offered his son advice
on being a king. He told him to be courageous
and strong and to walk in the ways of God. Good
advice for all of us.

*Loving God, help us walk in your ways so that
we might be the people you want us to be.*

Amen.

August 20

Jesus said to them, "I am the bread of life. Whoever comes to me will never be hungry, and whoever believes in me will never be thirsty.

JOHN 6:35

Our society values people who are self-sufficient. But as people of faith, we are asked to live lives that are God-sufficient. Saying, "I trust God," is easier than actually living into the trust.

Loving God, may our trust and faith in you deepen today in ways that are noticeable to you.

Amen.

August 21

*Now the word of the LORD came to me saying, "Before
I formed you in the womb I knew you, and before you
were born I consecrated you; I appointed you a prophet
to the nations." Then I said, "Ah, Lord GOD! Truly I
do not know how to speak, for I am only a boy."*

JEREMIAH 1:4–6

Jeremiah exclaims that he is only a boy, but in the
verses that follow, God reminds Jeremiah
wherever he goes and whatever he does, God will
always be with him. It is good to begin each day
with a reminder that our God is a steadfast and
enduring presence in all of our lives.

*Almighty God, through you, all is possible.
Help us as we lean on your presence to serve
those who come before us.*

Amen.

August 22

Be appalled, O heavens, at this, be shocked, be utterly desolate, says the LORD, for my people have committed two evils; they have forsaken me, the fountain of living water, and dug out cisterns for themselves, cracked cisterns that can hold no water.

JEREMIAH 2:12–13

This passage reminds us that when we rely solely on ourselves, we often find that we are our own worst enemies. Pray today that we can come to a deeper, more trusting relationship with God.

Almighty God, we want you at the center of our lives, but often on our terms. Help us release our lives into your care.

Amen.

August 23

*Bless the L*ORD*, O my soul, and all that is within me,
bless his holy name. Bless the L*ORD*, O my soul, and do
not forget all his benefits—who forgives all your
iniquity, who heals all your diseases, who redeems
your life from the Pit, who crowns you with steadfast
love and mercy, who satisfies you with good as long as
you live so that your youth is renewed like the eagle's.*

PSALM 103:1–5

Jesus said we must become as children. This
passage suggests that one way we become as
children is to let God permeate our lives in such a
complete way that our youth is renewed.

*Gracious God, help us open our hearts fully so
that you can enter our lives completely.*

Amen.

August 24

*The word that came to Jeremiah from the LORD:
"Come, go down to the potter's house, and there I
will let you hear my words." So I went to the
potter's house, and there he was working at his
wheel. The vessel he was making of clay was
spoiled in the potter's hand, and he reworked it
into another vessel, as seemed good to him.*

JEREMIAH 18:1–4

Like the potter at his wheel, God is constantly at
work in us. Even when we turn away from God
at different times in our lives, we can always return
to our faith, knowing that God's creative plan can
be reworked in us once we return.

*Steadfast God, help us always to place you
first so that your will for us will be done.*

Amen.

August 25

"Do not be afraid, little flock, for it is your Father's good pleasure to give you the kingdom. Sell your possessions, and give alms. Make purses for yourselves that do not wear out, an unfailing treasure in heaven, where no thief comes near and no moth destroys. For where your treasure is, there your heart will be also."

LUKE 12:32–34

Today, we are reminded that we should not lose hope. God remains steadfast, and we should place our trust in God and move boldly into our future as people of faith.

Steadfast and loving God, give us strength and courage to place our full trust in you.

Amen.

August 26

Now faith is the assurance of things hoped for, the conviction of things not seen. Indeed, by faith our ancestors received approval. By faith we understand that the worlds were prepared by the word of God, so that what is seen was made from things that are not visible.

HEBREWS 11:1–3

Life doesn't come with a set of one-size-fits-all directions. Yet we know that if hope is present in our lives, even if just a teaspoon, our ability to face life's challenges will be better. Helping people find or even rediscover hope in their lives can be life changing work for both the giver and receiver.

Loving God, help us be instillers of hope for your people whom we meet this and every day.

Amen.

August 27

The LORD brought Abram outside and said, "Look toward heaven and count the stars, if you are able to count them." Then he said to him, "So shall your descendants be." And he believed the LORD; and the LORD reckoned it to him as righteousness.

GENESIS 15:5–6

We live as people limited in our abilities and our vision. Yet the Scripture today reminds us that God is not bound by the limits we know. Our God is boundless—a hard concept for a limited mind to comprehend.

Almighty God, we cannot comprehend your knowledge of us, but we ask this day to catch a glimpse of ourselves as you see us.

Amen.

August 28

Jesus said to his disciples, "But who do you say that I am?" Simon Peter answered, "You are the Messiah, the Son of the living God." And Jesus answered him, "Blessed are you Simon son of Jonah! For flesh and blood has not revealed this to you, but my Father in heaven. And I tell you, you are Peter, and on this rock I will build my church, and the gates of Hades will not prevail against it."

MATTHEW 16:15–18

Abram became Abraham. Jacob became Israel. And now Simon becomes Peter (*petra* is Greek for "rock"). Transformational moments in the faith life of these leaders are marked by change—identity change, name change, responsibility change. Our faith should change us in ways that transform us, too.

Almighty God, help us find our calling, and then help us live into that vision.

Amen.

August 29

Now Israel loved Joseph more than any other of his children, because he was the son of his old age; and he made him a long robe with sleeves. But when his brothers saw that their father loved him more than all his brothers, they hated him, and could not speak peaceably to him.

GENESIS 37:3–4

God renamed Jacob, Israel, and this is the beginning of the story of the "amazing technicolor dreamcoat" Joseph. Like his father Jacob, Joseph was the youngest son, and despite Jewish tradition of the time which placed much honor on the firstborn, God is going to work through the youngest son again.

Gracious and wise God, you can work wonders through each of us. Continue to nudge us so we will always do your will.

Amen.

August 30

So Jacob said to Joseph "Go now, and see if it is well with your brothers and with the flock; and bring word back to me." … They saw him from a distance, and before he came near to them, they conspired to kill him. They said to one another, "Here comes this dreamer."

GENESIS 37:14, 18—19

I couldn't help but think of the words from John Lennon's song "Imagine." Lennon invites people into a bigger dream of what the world might be if we all lived as one.

Loving God, today we simply pray for peace—peace at home, peace at work, peace throughout the world.

Amen.

August 31

"God sent me before you to preserve life. For the famine has been in the land these two years; and there are five more years in which there will be neither plowing nor harvest. God sent me before you to preserve for you a remnant on earth, and to keep alive for you many survivors."

GENESIS 45:5–7

Joseph was not angry at his brothers because he saw God's hand as directing all the events leading up the moment we just read. Joseph had a keen sense of God's presence in his life. Think for a moment about how you sense God's active presence in your life.

Loving God, we thank you for your presence in our lives. Direct us so we can be the people you want us to be.

Amen.

September

A volunteer doctor works in the Clinic.

September 1

Are any among you sick? They should call for the elders of the church and have them pray over them, anointing them with oil in the name of the Lord.

JAMES 5:14

The Church Health Center opened on September 1, 1987, and we have been led by this passage since then. It calls the church to task in providing for our sick brothers and sisters through both spiritual means (prayer) and physical means (anointing)—healing people in body and spirit using both our bodies and our spirits.

Gracious God, help us be fully present for the people we meet today. May we be a healing presence for each person.

Amen.

September 2

Hear this, you that trample on the needy, and bring to ruin the poor of the land, saying, "When will the new moon be over so that we may sell grain; and the sabbath, so that we may offer wheat for sale? We will make the ephah small and the shekel great, and practice deceit with false balances, buying the poor for silver and the needy for a pair of sandals, and selling the sweepings of the wheat."

AMOS 8:4–6

An ephah was a unit of measure about the size of a bushel, and a shekel was likely referring to weight. The prophet is chastising those who anxiously await the end of Sabbath observances, so that they might get back to selling their wheat in less than bushel quantities at bushel prices, placing money and self ahead of God.

Almighty God, forgive us when our focus strays from doing your work in this world.

Amen.

September 3

*Have mercy on me, O God, according to your steadfast
love; according to your abundant mercy blot out my
transgressions. Wash me thoroughly from my iniquity,
and cleanse me from my sin.*

PSALM 51:1–2

Each of us has hurt someone unintentionally in
ways that might have had significant
consequences for the one hurt. Psalm 51 creates a
beautiful prayer of repentance and renewal.

*You desire truth in the inward being;
therefore teach us wisdom in our secret
hearts. Create in us clean hearts, O God,
and put new and right spirits within us.*

Amen.

September 4

Then the LORD came down in the cloud and spoke to Moses, and took some of the spirit that was on him and put it on the seventy elders; and when the spirit rested upon them, they prophesied.

NUMBERS 11:25

This verse provides a wonderful image of God taking a bit of Moses' spirit and passing it onto others so that they can be stronger. As you interact with people today, consider this passage, and try to leave a bit of your spirit behind with them so that they can be stronger.

Almighty God, help us be better instruments of your will as we work with your children today.

Amen.

September 5

For to me, living is Christ and dying is gain. If I am to live in the flesh, that means fruitful labor for me; and I do not know which I prefer. I am hard pressed between the two: my desire is to depart and be with Christ, for that is far better; but to remain in the flesh is more necessary for you.

PHILIPPIANS 1:21–24

Paul's reason for living is to help his fellow believers as they grow in their understanding of God. We cannot live individually as if we are islands. We are born of one God, and we must care for each other as the family members we are.

Gracious God, we have independent spirits, but you remind us of our dependence on you and on each other. Help us to serve one another.

Amen.

September 6

O give thanks to the LORD, call on his name, make known his deeds among the peoples. Sing to him, sing praises to him; tell of all his wonderful works.

PSALM 105:1–2

I believe our actions should be outward expressions of our faith. This Scripture reminds us that we should also tell others how we see God active in the world.

Ever-present God, we witness your creative presence each day. Help us share that witness with others.

Amen.

September 7

*There was once a man in the land of Uz whose name was Job. That man was blameless and upright, one who feared God and turned away from evil ... Then Satan answered the L*ord*, "Skin for skin! All that people have they will give to save their lives."*

JOB 1:1; 2:4

According to Satan's worldview, we are self-centered to a fault, yet in my world, I see people giving of themselves for others every day. God calls us to sacrificial love for one another, and when I look at how my family, friends, and coworkers act toward one another, I see daily examples of sacrificial love practiced by seemingly ordinary people.

Steadfast God, help us be strong people of faith who are always aware of your presence with us.

Amen.

September 8

*"There is a boy here who has five barley loaves and
two fish. But what are they among so many
people?" Jesus said, "Make the people sit down."
Now there was a great deal of grass in the place; so
they sat down, about five thousand in all. Then
Jesus took the loaves, and when he had given
thanks, he distributed them to those who were
seated; so also the fish, as much as they wanted.*

JOHN 6:9–11

This is the only account of the feeding of the 5,000
that identifies "a boy" as the one who had
brought the food that was then distributed to all. It
seems that a child would be an unlikely central
character in one of Jesus' most remembered miracles,
but as with David, we are once again reminded that
God can work through anyone, even us.

*God of mystery, guide us to stretch beyond
our own limitations through you.*

Amen.

September 9

*I am reminded of your sincere faith, a faith that lived
first in your grandmother Lois and your mother
Eunice and now, I am sure, lives in you. For this
reason, I remind you to rekindle the gift of God that is
within you through the laying on of my hands...*

2 TIMOTHY 1:5–6

Paul speaks of the spiritual inheritance Timothy received from his mother and grandmother, and Paul asks him to reclaim it. Who are the people of faith in your life who have blessed you? Give thanks for them today.

*Almighty God, for encouraging our
faith in you, we give thanks this day for
all those whose lives bore witness to
your role in their lives.*

Amen.

September 10

*When evening came, his disciples went down to the
sea, got into a boat, and started across the sea to
Capernaum. It was now dark, and Jesus had not yet
come to them. The sea became rough because a strong
wind was blowing. When they had rowed about three
or four miles, they saw Jesus walking on the sea and
coming near the boat, and they were terrified. But he
said to them, "It is I; do not be afraid."*

JOHN 6:16–20

I take comfort in knowing that the disciples weren't
always pictures of unfailing faith. Like us, their
ability to trust, to have faith, wasn't always complete.
Just as Jesus said to his disciples, he stands by us
saying, "Do not be afraid." May our faith grow to
trust those words at all times.

*Steadfast God, your faith in us is greater than
our faith in you. Work within us so that our
faith in you deepens.*

Amen.

September 11

*Then Peter came to Jesus and said to him, "Lord,
if another member of the church sins against me,
how often should I forgive? As many as seven
times?" Jesus said to him, "Not seven times, but
I tell you, seventy-seven times."*

MATTHEW 18:21–22

In the parable that follows these verses, Jesus reminds us that God is generously forgiving of us. In return, we should be generously forgiving of each other. I would hesitate to say I have always been generously forgiving. But I would say that when I have both sought and offered forgiveness, I have come away feeling healed.

*Gracious God, give us strength and courage to
be the forgiving people you want us to be.*

Amen.

September 12

*My joy is gone, grief is upon me, my heart is
sick ... For the hurt of my poor people I am
hurt, I mourn, and dismay has taken hold of
me. Is there no balm in Gilead? Is there no
physician there? Why then has the health of
my poor people not been restored?*

<small>JEREMIAH 8:18, 21–22</small>

I sometimes think we live in the Age of Me. We are encouraged to look perfect, get rich and out-compete one another. But I believe that as people of faith, we are called to live out that faith in loving community with one another.

*Gracious God, help us better cry out for
one another as we seek to do your will
today and every day.*

Amen.

September 13

*The LORD said to Moses, "Go down at once! Your
people, whom you brought up out of the land of
Egypt, have acted perversely; they have been quick
to turn aside from the way that I commanded
them; They have cast for themselves an image of a
calf, and have worshiped it and sacrificed to it, and
said, 'These are your gods, O Israel, who brought
you up out of the land of Egypt!'"*

EXODUS 32:7–8

I don't think of us as patient people in general. To
varying degrees, we want life to go our way when
we want it. But God's time may not be our time.

*Gracious God, grant each of us more
patience so that we might see your plan
unfold before us.*

Amen.

September 14

*"Listen to another parable. There was a
landowner who planted a vineyard, put a
fence around it, dug a wine press in it, and
built a watchtower. Then he leased it to
tenants and went to another country. When
the harvest time had come, he sent his slaves
to the tenants to collect his produce. But the
tenants seized his slaves and beat one, killed
another, and stoned another.*

MATTHEW 21:33–35

As tenant-managers of God's creation, we are
the caretakers of God's world and each other.
With that said, it is too easy for us to become
destructive members of God's creation, as is the
case of the tenants in this parable. Today, consider
ways you are engaged in tending God's creation.

*Trusting God, you place much responsibility
in our hands, and we often fall short. Help us
to be the people you want us to be.*

Amen.

September 15

Say to those who are of a fearful heart, "Be strong, do not fear! Here is your God. He will come with vengeance, with terrible recompense. He will come to save you." Then the eyes of the blind shall be opened, and the ears of the deaf unstopped; then the lame shall leap like a deer, and the tongues of the speechless sing for joy.

ISAIAH 35:4–6

In this passage, the presence of God is linked to physical healing—the blind see, the deaf hear, the lame leap, and the mute sing. The kingdom of God brings miracles that defy our expectations!

Almighty God, may those we see today sense your presence in us so that we can be a source of healing for them.

Amen.

September 16

Remember the sabbath day, and keep it holy. Six days you shall labor and do all your work.

EXODUS 20:8–9

We live in a 24/7/365 world that rarely encourages us to slow down. In this passage God reminds us to rest and renew our spirits on a regular basis.

God of our renewal, rest and work, we come to you as a priority-challenged people. Thank you for your unending grace.

Amen.

September 17

But if you have envy and selfish ambition in your hearts, do not be boastful and false to the truth ... For where there is bitter envy and selfish ambition, there will also be disorder and wickedness of every kind.

JAMES 3:14, 16

The image this passage gave me was of two people in a rowboat, each rowing with no regard to the other. The rowboat simply spins in a circle, never moving forward. I see this passage as saying that envy and selfishness can create disorder in our lives that, like the rowboat, can cause us to circle aimlessly.

Loving God, help us lead lives focused outwardly toward one another and upwardly toward you.

Amen.

September 18

You shall not murder. You shall not commit adultery. You shall not steal. You shall not bear false witness against your neighbor.

EXODUS 20:13–16

The first commandments instruct us on how to relate to God. These commandments instruct us on how we should relate to each other. To me, they tell us to respect the lives, loves, property and reputations of our neighbors.

Loving God, help us to love you with all our heart and all our mind, and help us to love our neighbors as ourselves.

Amen.

September 19

*The Lord is gracious and merciful, slow to anger
and abounding in steadfast love.*

PSALM 145:8

Remember Jesus's directive in Scripture to forgive someone who has sinned against you not seven times but 77 times (Matthew 18:21–22)? We are asked to treat one another as God treats us—with mercy, patience and love.

*Loving God, your generosity toward us is
often unmerited. Help us treat one another as
brothers and sisters and not as strangers.*

Amen.

September 20

Those who eat must not despise those who abstain,
and those who abstain must not pass judgment on
those who eat; for God has welcomed them. Some
judge one day to be better than another, while others
judge all days to be alike. Let all be fully convinced
in their own minds. Those who observe the day,
observe it in honor of the Lord. Also, those who eat,
eat in honor of the Lord, since they give thanks to
God; while those who abstain, abstain in honor of the
Lord and give thanks to God.

ROMANS 14:3, 5–6

I can't help but think how different our communities
and our world might be if we could collectively
focus on the God who binds us together rather than
the details which separate us.

God of all, be with us throughout this day.
Keep us mindful of the breadth of your
kingdom and all your children in it.

Amen.

September 21

But turning and looking at his disciples, Jesus
rebuked Peter and said, "Get behind me,
Satan! For you are setting your mind not on
divine things but on human things."

MARK 8:33

We set priorities every day. I have a planner that I use each day to keep me on track with my to-dos at work. This passage reminds us that our daily tasks should include those things which bring us closer to God.

Loving God, help us set our priorities on those
things which bring glory to you.

Amen.

September 22

The thought of my affliction and my homelessness is wormwood and gall! My soul continually thinks of it and is bowed down within me. But this I call to mind, and therefore I have hope: The steadfast love of the LORD never ceases, his mercies never come to an end; they are new every morning, great is your faithfulness.

LAMENTATIONS 3:19–23

One of my favorite hymns, "Great is Thy Faithfulness," is based on verses 22 and 23 of this passage. Despite the sadness over the loss of Jerusalem, the writer continues to give glory and honor to God, acknowledging as in the hymn, "Morning by morning new mercies I see."

Steadfast God, while we struggle with short attention spans, your love for us is never-ending. Thank you for this day and all the possibilities for service it brings.

Amen.

September 23

For the love of money is a root of all kinds of evil,
and in their eagerness to be rich some have wandered
away from the faith and pierced themselves with
many pains. But as for you, man of God, shun all
this; pursue righteousness, godliness, faith, love,
endurance, gentleness. Fight the good fight of the
faith; take hold of the eternal life, to which you were
called and for which you made the good confession in
the presence of many witnesses.

1 TIMOTHY 6:10–12

Paul instructs Timothy that it is easy to place
money and other pursuits before God,
sometimes with disastrous results. Paul suggests
that the path of faith won't always be an easy one,
but Paul assures him, and us, that the life of faith is
ultimately worth the effort.

Understanding God, help us to be the
disciples you want us to be.

Amen.

September 24

*Happy are those whose help is the God of Jacob,
whose hope is in the LORD their God, who made
heaven and earth, the sea, and all that is in them;
who keeps faith forever; who executes justice for
the oppressed; who gives food to the hungry. The
LORD sets the prisoners free; the LORD opens the
eyes of the blind. The LORD lifts up those who are
bowed down; the LORD loves the righteous.*

PSALM 146:5–8

The psalmist assures us that our creator God feeds us, heals us, and frees us. God also opens our eyes and helps us stand up straight. The psalmist implores us to place our trust in God, "who keeps faith forever."

*Faithful God, you have more faith in us
than we have in ourselves. Help us see
ourselves as you see us.*

Amen.

September 25

You who live in the shelter of the Most High, who abide in the shadow of the Almighty, will say to the LORD, "My refuge and my fortress; my God, in whom I trust." For he will deliver you from the snare of the fowler and from the deadly pestilence; he will cover you with his pinions, and under his wings you will find refuge.

PSALM 91:1–4

Pinion, in this context, refers to the strongest part of the bird's wing where the bones are located. The psalmist is assuring us that God remains with us always, even in times of great trouble.

Steadfast God, you promise you are always with us. Help us be more trusting of you.

Amen.

September 26

"Which of you, having a hundred sheep and losing one of them, does not leave the ninety-nine in the wilderness and go after the one that is lost until he finds it? When he has found it, he lays it on his shoulders and rejoices."

LUKE 15:4–5

In today's Scripture, Jesus speaks to the Pharisees and scribes, pointing to the personal relationship God has with each one of us. God will find us even when we are lost and alone.

Steadfast and loving God, you care about each of us. Help us become the people you want us to be.

Amen.

September 27

*But Moses implored the L*ORD *his God, and said, "O*
*L*ORD*, why does your wrath burn hot against your*
people, whom you brought out of the land of Egypt
with great power and with a mighty hand? … Turn
from your fierce wrath; change your mind and do
*not bring disaster on your people." … And the L*ORD
changed his mind about the disaster that he planned
to bring on his people.

EXODUS 32:11–12, 14

This passage finds Moses imploring God to take a different path than the one he has in mind. While so many of our prayers end with "thy will be done," this passage encourages us not only to pray for one another but also to pray boldly.

Almighty God, thank you for the
parental love you offer, for the steadfast
love and understanding that comes from
knowing our innermost selves.

Amen.

September 28

Jesus said to the chief priests and the elders, "I will ask
you one question; if you tell me the answer, then I will
also tell you by what authority I do these things. Did
the baptism of John come from heaven or was it of
human origin?" And they argued with one another,
"If we say, 'From heaven,' he will say to us, 'Why then
did you not believe him?' But if we say, 'Of human
origin,' we are afraid of the crowd; for all regard John
as a prophet." So they answered Jesus, "We do not
know." And he said to them, "Neither will I tell you
by what authority I am doing these things."

MATTHEW 21:24–27

The leaders face a conundrum, a situation familiar
to many of us. What our faith demands of us is
not always clear, but we are asked to walk forward
faithfully, knowing God is forgiving when we misstep.

Gracious God, help us see the path
you want us to take.

Amen.

September 29

The Lord said to Moses, "Go on ahead of the people, and take some of the elders of Israel with you; take in your hand the staff with which you struck the Nile, and go. I will be standing there in front of you on the rock at Horeb. Strike the rock, and water will come out of it, so that the people may drink." Moses did so, in the sight of the elders of Israel.

Exodus 17:5–6

God provides. It is a simple sentence, yet it is one shrouded in much mystery. I imagine few of us will have such a dramatic example as that offered the Israelites in today's Scripture, but I do hope each of us will be able to sense God's active presence in our lives.

Provider God, help us to sense your presence in our lives. May we be instruments of your provisions to others in our work today.

Amen.

September 30

But as for me, I walk in my integrity; redeem me, and be gracious to me. My foot stands on level ground; in the great congregation I will bless the LORD.

PSALM 26:11–12

When I read this Scripture, I thought of helping someone stand up who has fallen. I take their forearm in my hand, then I plant my feet firmly and evenly on the ground so I won't slip as they rise up. Similarly, God's spirit provides a sort of level ground for us so that we can walk truthfully and honestly.

Almighty God, give us strength to meet the challenges of this day.

Amen.

October

Playing in the Child Life area of Wellness.

October 1

*But Jesus said to them, "You do not know
what you are asking. Are you able to drink the
cup that I drink, or be baptized with the
baptism that I am baptized with?"*

MARK 10:38

Years ago, WWJD bracelets asked us to consider,
"What would Jesus do?" I make decisions
throughout the day, but most of them are automatic.
This passage reminds us that we should consider
our faith in each decision, even the smallest ones.

*Loving God, help us be more mindful of your
will both for us and for your kingdom.*

Amen.

October 2

*But it is not so among you; but whoever
wishes to become great among you must be
your servant, and whoever wishes to be first
among you must be slave of all.*

MARK 10:43–44

I am not sure there is a more clear statement of
our relationship to one another than that found
in this passage. We are to serve one another.

*Gracious God, we live in community with one
another, but we often ignore our neighbor.
Help us be the neighbors you want us to be.*

Amen.

October 3

The apostles said to the Lord, "Increase our faith!" The Lord replied, "If you had faith the size of a mustard seed, you could say to this mulberry tree, 'Be uprooted and planted in the sea,' and it would obey you.

LUKE 17:5–6

While it is easy to speak of the deep and abiding faith of prophets and psalmists, Jesus reminds us in Luke today that great faith is not needed. Just faith.

Loving God, instill in us an enduring faith that will assure us throughout the trials and tribulations of our life.

Amen.

October 4

And you became imitators of us and of the Lord,
for in spite of persecution, you received the word
with joy inspired by the Holy Spirit, so that you
became an example to all the believers in
Macedonia and in Achaia.

1 THESSALONIANS 1:6–7

It's a tall order to live your life as an imitation of the Lord. For all those times I fall woefully short, I am thankful for God's abundant grace. Our faith should make us distinctive in ways that can inspire others.

Steadfast God of Grace, help us to be
better examples of your love and to care
for all of your creation.

Amen.

October 5

*When the people saw that Moses delayed to come
down from the mountain, the people gathered
around Aaron, and said to him, "Come, make gods
for us, who shall go before us; as for this Moses, the
man who brought us up out of the land of Egypt, we
do not know what has become of him." Aaron said to
them, "Take off the gold rings that are on the ears of
your wives, your sons and your daughters, and
bring them to me." ... He took the gold from them,
formed it in a mold, and cast an image of a calf..."*

EXODUS 32:1–2, 4

Like the Israelites in the passage above, many of
us are impatient. We will say, "God's time is
perfect time," but what we really want is for God
to be on our time table. Today, we pray for patience
and wisdom.

*Gracious God, grant us patience and wisdom,
this day and everyday.*

Amen.

October 6

When they told David, "Uriah did not go down to his house," David said to Uriah, "You have just come from a journey. Why did you not go down to your house?" Uriah said to David, "The ark and Israel and Judah remain in booths; and my lord Joab and the servants of my lord are camping in the open field; shall I then go to my house, to eat and to drink, and to lie with my wife? As you live, and as your soul lives, I will not do such a thing."

2 SAMUEL 11:10–11

Uriah returns from battle, but he refuses to stay at his home or to see his wife because of his loyalty to his colleagues who are still on the battlefield. Do you have a Uriah in your life? Someone who will be loyal and committed to you?

Gracious God, thank you for giving us loyal friends and family on whom we can rely.

Amen.

October 7

*Every high priest chosen from among mortals is put in
charge of things pertaining to God on their behalf, to
offer gifts and sacrifices for sins. He is able to deal
gently with the ignorant and wayward, since he
himself is subject to weakness.*

HEBREWS 5:1–2

We are all subject to weakness, even the high
priests among us. This passage reminds me
of how important it is for us to be slow to judge
others, being forever mindful of our own
shortcomings.

*Understanding God, we are all related as
your children. Help us to look at each other
with the understanding often reserved
for blood relatives.*

Amen.

October 8

Mighty King, lover of justice, you have established equity; you have executed justice and righteousness in Jacob. Extol the LORD our God; worship at his footstool. Holy is he!

PSALM 99:4–5

God loves justice. To be just people, we have to be fair in our dealings with one another. We have to be honest, and we must be truthful and reliable. Today, we ask God to help us be justice-makers.

Merciful God, may our actions today help bring justice to the world. Help us be fair, evenhanded and honest in all we do.

Amen.

October 9

*Finally, beloved, whatever is true, whatever is
honorable, whatever is just, whatever is pure, whatever
is pleasing, whatever is commendable, if there is any
excellence and if there is anything worthy of praise,
think about these things. Keep on doing the things you
have learned and received and heard and seen in me,
and the God of peace will be with you.*

PHILIPPIANS 4:8–9

I n the verses prior to these, we are asked to be
gentle with each other and not to worry about
anything. We are assured that our God of peace will
always be with us.

*Loving God, help us always to be of right mind
so that we might be the people you need us to
be: gentle, patient and supportive.*

Amen.

October 10

Many are the afflictions of the righteous, but the LORD rescues them from them all. He keeps their bones; not one of them will be broken.

P SALM 34:19–20

L ong after our flesh has gone, our bones will remain. This passage reminds us that God's love and care for us transcends this world. While our lives will have pains and trials, we are never left to face those challenges alone.

Steadfast God, thank you for remaining by our side at all times.

Amen.

October 11

Jesus' disciples were greatly astounded and said to one another, "Then who can be saved?" Jesus looked at them and said, "For mortals it is impossible, but not for God; for God all things are possible."

MARK 10:26–27

Nothing is impossible for God. God remains a steadfast presence in our lives. God does not abandon us. God works in us and through us to build God's kingdom.

Steadfast God, give us ears to hear your still small voice in our lives so that we might build the kingdom you envision.

Amen.

October 12

*Indeed, the word of God is living and active, sharper
than any two-edged sword, piercing until it divides
soul from spirit, joints from marrow; it is able to judge
the thoughts and intentions of the heart.*

HEBREWS 4:12

I take great comfort in knowing that God is living
and active in my life. This means that our actions
toward others can be an outward manifestation of
God's real-time presence in our lives.

*Ever-present God, work within each of us
today so that the people we meet can see your
face being reflected back.*

Amen.

October 13

*You shall know that I am in the midst of Israel, and
that I, the LORD, am your God and there is no other.
And my people shall never again be put to shame.
Then afterward I will pour out my spirit on all flesh;
your sons and your daughters shall prophesy, your old
men shall dream dreams, and your young men shall
see visions. Even on the male and female slaves, in
those days, I will pour out my spirit.*

JOEL 2:27–29

Anticipate the impossible! Expect the
unexpected! We worship a limitless God who
loves all of us.

*Almighty God, open our eyes and our minds
to your love that knows no limits.*

Amen.

October 14

I lift up my eyes to the hills—from where will my help come? My help comes from the LORD, who made heaven and earth ... The LORD will keep you from all evil; he will keep your life. The LORD will keep your going out and your coming in from this time on and forevermore.

PSALM 121:1–2, 7–9

Part of the addiction recovery process involves submitting oneself to God, of crying out, "Help me, Lord!" But crying out for God's help and guidance is not reserved for those in need of recovery from a powerful addiction. Psalm 121 provides guidance for all of us.

Creator God, help us sense your unending presence in our lives so that we will be better able to lean on you.

Amen.

October 15

*They exchanged the glory of God for the image of an ox
that eats grass. They forgot God, their Savior, who had
done great things in Egypt, wondrous works in the
land of Ham, and awesome deeds by the Red Sea.
Therefore God said he would destroy them—had not
Moses, his chosen one, stood in the breach before him,
to turn away his wrath from destroying them.*

PSALM 106:20–23

I love that phrase "stood in the breach before him."
Moses pleaded with God to spare his people after
they created the gold calf, and God listened. Is there
someone in your life for whom you should stand
in the breach before God? Pray a special prayer for
that person today.

*Merciful God, you already know the
people in our lives who are in trouble.
Be with each of them today, so that they
may be comforted by your presence.*

Amen.

October 16

O give thanks to the LORD, for he is good; for his steadfast love endures forever.

PSALM 107:1

This verse reminds us that God's love for us is unwavering and unfaltering. God loves us more surely than we love ourselves.

Loving God, we thank you for being resolute in your love for us. Work in us this day to help further your kingdom.

Amen.

October 17

*As Jesus and his disciples and a large crowd
were leaving Jericho, Bartimaeus son of Timaeus, a
blind beggar, was sitting by the roadside. When
he heard that it was Jesus of Nazareth, he began to
shout out and say, "Jesus, Son of David, have
mercy on me!" Many sternly ordered Bartimaeus
to be quiet, but he cried out even more loudly,
"Son of David, have mercy on me!"*

MARK 10:46–48

When I first read this passage, what struck me
was not that Bartimaeus cried out the first
time but that he cried out the second time as people
were trying to silence him. Just as Bartimaeus cried
out for his healing, we too have to advocate for our
own healing.

*Healer God, give strength to our voice so that
we can find the healing we need.*

Amen.

October 18

He was trying to see who Jesus was, but on account of the crowd he could not, because he was short in stature. So he ran ahead and climbed a sycamore tree to see him, because he was going to pass that way. When Jesus came to the place, he looked up and said to him, "Zacchaeus, hurry and come down; for I must stay at your house today."

LUKE 19:3–5

I often find myself in a situation where I am wishing I knew the right words to say to offer comfort, support or praise. Zacchaeus, who reportedly says nothing before being noticed by Jesus, reminds us of the truth of the adage that actions often do speak louder than words.

Gracious God, may our actions and our words toward one another reflect our faith in you.

Amen.

October 19

As for me, I am already being poured out as a
libation, and the time of my departure has come.
I have fought the good fight, I have finished the race,
I have kept the faith.

2 TIMOTHY 4:6–7

I find Paul's race analogy very helpful. First, Paul says he finished the race, but he didn't say he won the race. Participation, not victory, is key. Second, I think of the stitch I get in my side after the simplest exertion. The race of faith in which we run can be difficult, even painful, at times.

Steadfast God, in our race of faith,
help us to know your presence so that
we may continue to draw on your
strength when we are faltering.

Amen.

October 20

"Two men went up to the temple to pray, one a Pharisee and the other a tax collector ... But the tax collector, standing far off, would not even look up to heaven, but was beating his breast and saying, 'God, be merciful to me, a sinner!' I tell you, this man went down to his home justified rather than the other; for all who exalt themselves will be humbled, but all who humble themselves will be exalted."

LUKE 18:10, 13–14

"Keep things in perspective," is advice often given to one who is not seeing the whole picture, when one is missing the forest for the trees. Today's passage reminds us to keep ourselves in perspective, too.

Loving and patient God, help us as we work to walk humbly with you.

Amen.

October 21

*When the man saw that he did not prevail against
Jacob, he struck him on the hip socket; and Jacob's hip
was put out of joint as he wrestled with him. Then he
said, "Let me go, for the day is breaking." But Jacob
said, "I will not let you go, unless you bless me."*

GENESIS 32:25–26

"You missed your calling," is a phrase many
of us have heard from well-meaning friends.
No doubt some of us have missed our calling. Some
of us have even wrestled with God to avoid living
into God's plan for us.

*Loving God, we don't always understand your
will for us, but we humbly ask you to bless our
efforts this and every day.*

Amen.

October 22

O LORD, how long shall I cry for help, and you will not listen? Or cry to you, "Violence!" and you will not save? Why do you make me see wrong-doing and look at trouble? Destruction and violence are before me; strife and contention arise.

HABAKKUK 1:2–3

Yes, this is another prophet seemingly frustrated with God by what he sees happening to his brothers and sisters. And yet, I can't help but think how much better the world would be if more of us cried out to God to help us like Habakkuk is doing in the passage.

Almighty God, strengthen us so that we can better help those less fortunate among us.

Amen.

October 23

Jesus stood still and said, "Call him here."
And they called the blind man, saying to him,
"Take heart; get up, he is calling you."
MARK 10:49

A blind man sitting on the side of the road calls out to Jesus for help, and the disciples try to silence him. "Don't bother the teacher," they seem to be saying. This scene plays out with different characters repeatedly in Scripture. People walking beside Jesus, hearing him firsthand, fail to understand him. Jesus asks us to care for one another and to be healing presences for one another.

Patient God, we live by agendas and habits
that are of our own making. Remain by us and
gently nudge us toward your will.

Amen.

October 24

*Wash yourselves; make yourselves clean; remove the
evil of your doings from before my eyes; cease to do
evil, learn to do good; seek justice, rescue the
oppressed, defend the orphan, plead for the widow.*

ISAIAH 1:16–17

Isaiah is offering the word of the Lord to the people
of Sodom and Gomorrah in today's passage.
Earlier in the passage, God seems to scoff at their
sacrifices and burnt offerings. God is telling them
to care for those less fortunate among them.

*Loving God, give us eyes to see the needs of
those around us, and give us the wisdom to
offer substantive help.*

Amen.

October 25

When Jesus saw the ten lepers, he said to them, "Go and show yourselves to the priests." And as they went, they were made clean. Then one of them, when he saw he was healed, turned back, praising God with a loud voice. He prostrated himself at Jesus' feet and thanked him. He was a Samaritan.

LUKE 17:14–16

The Samaritan is the only one of the ten who shows his appreciation for the healing he was granted. This passage reminds each of us to adopt an attitude of gratitude both for those around us and for God.

Patient God, you offer us so much, yet so often you get so little from us in return. Give us more grateful hearts.

Amen.

October 26

Naaman, commander of the army of the king of Aram, was a great man and in high favor with his master, because by him the LORD had given victory to Aram. The man, though a mighty warrior, suffered from leprosy.

2 KINGS 5:1

Naaman suffered from a disease that made most others of his time outcasts. Despite living in a time of more enlightenment about disease and disease transmission, we still make outcasts of some of God's children who are suffering.

Gracious God, keep us mindful of our own frailties, and help us to be more compassionate to those who are suffering.

Amen.

October 27

"And the second commandment is like it: 'You shall love your neighbor as yourself.'"
MATTHEW 22:39

I have lived on my street for over 20 years. In reading this familiar verse, I am struck by the fact I barely know many of my neighbors. To be sure, I harbor no ill will toward any of them, but it is hard to love your neighbors if you don't make an effort to get to know them.

God of Peace, it is easy for us to live under a veil of indifference toward our neighbors. Help open our hearts to one another.

Amen.

October 28

*Paul, Silvanus, and Timothy, To the church of the
Thessalonians in God the Father and the Lord Jesus
Christ: Grace to you and peace. We always give thanks
to God for all of you and mention you in our prayers,
constantly remembering before our God and Father
your work of faith and labor of love and steadfastness
of hope in our Lord Jesus Christ.*

1 Thessalonians 1:1–3

Is praying for others part of your daily routine?
Paul clearly states that he prays to God, constantly
remembering the works of faith of his Thessalonian
brothers and sisters.

*Gracious God, we ask you to be with each
person we see today, and we ask a special
blessing for those brothers and sisters whose
faith serves as a testament to us and to others.*

Amen.

October 29

And Moses said to the LORD, "If your presence will not go, do not carry us up from here. For how shall it be known that I have found favor in your sight, I and your people, unless you go with us? In this way, we shall be distinct, I and your people, from every people on the face of the earth."

EXODUS 33:15–16

How does God's presence in your life make you distinct? Can people tell you are a person of faith from your actions toward them? Our faith can shine through as a testament to God through small things we do for one another—understanding touches, kind words, helping hands.

Gracious God, help our lives to be living testaments of your presence in our lives.

Amen.

October 30

Let your work be manifest to your servants, and your glorious power to their children. Let the favor of the LORD our God be upon us, and prosper for us the work of our hands — O prosper the work of our hands!

PSALM 90:16–17

In the 20 years I have worked at the Church Health Center, I have seen remarkable growth in both our organization, and in myself. I believe that God has prospered the work of our hands. I pray that you may know the same blessing.

Gracious God, may the work of our hands clearly show your work in us.

Amen.

October 31

*At my first defense no one came to my support, but all
deserted me. May it not be counted against them! But
the Lord stood by me and gave me strength, so that
through me the message might be fully proclaimed and
all the Gentiles might hear it.*

2 TIMOTHY 4:16–17

What a powerful statement of forgiveness Paul
is making in this passage today! We might
often feel alone in a time of need. Yet this passage
reminds us that God gives us strength for the journey.

*Gracious God, forgive us our trespasses as we
forgive those who trespass against us.*

Amen.

November

Knitting prayer shawls for people in need.

November 1

*Lead me in your truth, and teach me, for you are the
God of my salvation; for you I wait all day long.*

PSALM 25:5

Trust, even trust in God, must be cultivated
and developed over time. This passage asks
us to trust God as we are moving forward. As you
walk today, consider how you are allowing God
to lead you.

*Steadfast God, we want to go where you lead.
Help us to see your way for us.*

Amen.

November 2

For the L<small>ORD</small> has chosen Zion; he has desired it for his habitation: "This is my final resting place forever; here I will reside, for I have desired it. I will abundantly bless its provisions; I will satisfy its poor with bread. Its priests I will clothe with salvation, and its faithful will shout for joy.

P<small>SALM</small> 132:13–16

It is easy to think of abundance only in terms of monetary wealth. Yet abundance in this passage is associated with basic sustenance and joy-filled living that that comes with living close to God.

Gracious God, help us lead faith-centered lives so that we can experience life as fully as you intend for us.

Amen.

November 3

"As for these things that you see, the days will come when not one stone will be left upon another; all will be thrown down." They asked him, "Teacher, when will this be, and what will be the sign that this is about to take place?" And he said, "Beware that you are not led astray; for many will come in my name and say, 'I am he!' and 'The time is near!' Do not go after them."

LUKE 21:6–8

Have faith in our mighty and wondrous God! This passage reminds us to have faith in our faith, to trust our understanding of our faith amid the challenges that seek to pull that faith out from under us.

Steadfast God, give us strength and wisdom to be faithful servants to both you and one another.

Amen.

November 4

*Then the king will say to those at his right hand,
'Come, you that are blessed by my Father, inherit the
kingdom prepared for you from the foundation of the
world; for I was hungry and you gave me food, I was
thirsty and you gave me something to drink, I was a
stranger and you welcomed me, I was naked and you
gave me clothing, I was sick and you took care of me, I
was in prison and you visited me."*

MATTHEW 25:34–36

All of us are members of God's family. God is mysteriously yet intricately woven into each of us so that by serving each other, we are also serving God.

*Ever-present God, keep us mindful
that your children surround us. Help
us act toward them in ways that
reflect how we act toward you.*

Amen.

November 5

LORD, you have been our dwelling place in all generations. Before the mountains were brought forth, or ever you had formed the earth and the world, from everlasting to everlasting, you are God.

The image of God as our "dwelling place" helps me visualize how inseparable we are from God. There are times when we may feel alone, but God is always there. There are times when we may want to hide from God, but we can't hide from the God who was, is and always will be.

Creator God, we lift our eyes up to you and incline our ears to you. Lead us on paths that are pleasing to you.

Amen.

November 6

*Heaven and earth will pass away, but my words will
not pass away. But about that day or hour no one
knows, neither the angels in heaven, nor the Son, but
only the Father. Beware, keep alert; for you do not
know when the time will come.*

MARK 13:31–33

Just as God is faithful, we too are to be faithful at
all times. It challenges us to lead lives that
anticipate God's presence around every corner and
in every face.

*Gracious God, we don't know the day or
hour of your return, but we ask you for
strength today so that we will act in ways
that are true to your will.*

Amen.

November 7

But the widow said, "As the LORD your God lives,
I have nothing baked, only a handful of meal in a jar,
and a little oil in a jug; I am now gathering a couple
of sticks, so that I may go home and prepare it for
myself and my son, that we may eat it, and die."
Elijah said to her, … "For thus says the LORD the
God of Israel: The jar of meal will not be emptied
and the jug of oil will not fail until the day the LORD
sends rain on the earth."

1 KINGS 17:12, 14

I can only imagine the pain this widow must have felt as she was gathering those few sticks to prepare the final meal for her son. It is precisely at this moment that she is offered the chance to make a leap of faith, to have hope amidst her hopelessness. In our times of greatest need, may we hear God as clearly as she did.

Gracious God, give us ears that hear your voice.

Amen.

November 8

Now when these things begin to take place,
stand up and raise your heads, because your
redemption is drawing near.

LUKE 21:28

Lower your head as though you are in prayer, then raise your head as though you are seeing the glory of God. If this motion feels comfortable to you, repeat it today as you pray to God.

God of mystery, we raise our heads toward you
so that we can see you more clearly.

Amen.

November 9

Now may our God and Father himself and our Lord
Jesus direct our way to you.

1 THESSALONIANS 3:11

Prayers to God are often open-ended requests for direction. In today's passage, the apostle Paul is asking God to lead him to specific people. There is at least one person in your life who needs your presence. Consider that person and pray today that God will provide a way to lead you to him or her.

Merciful God, while we are trying to walk
where you lead, we ask today that you lead
us to this person who is weighing heavy
on our hearts and provide us a way to offer
this person comfort.

Amen.

November 10

To you, O Lord, I lift up my soul.
PSALM 25:1

Close your eyes and meditate on this brief passage. Repeat this passage raising your arms over your head each time. As you raise your arms, stretch your fingers wide as though you are holding tight to God's grace. Throughout the day, take a 15-second prayer break by repeating the passage to yourself four times.

Awesome God, we offer ourselves to your service this and every day.

Amen.

November 11

You will be made rich in every way so that you can be generous on every occasion, and through us your generosity will result in thanksgiving to God. This service that you perform is not only supplying the needs of God's people but is also overflowing in many expressions of thanks to God.

2 CORINTHIANS 9:11–12

As most of us do, I enjoy eating good food and wearing nice clothes. But when I bow my head at the table on Thanksgiving, what I am most thankful for are the family and friends who surround me. It is through these people that I often feel a sense of closeness to God.

Gracious God, thank you for friends and family and for the way we can see you through these precious relationships.

Amen.

November 12

*Be on guard so that your hearts are not weighed down
with dissipation and drunkenness and the worries of
this life, and that day does not catch you unexpectedly.*

LUKE 21:34

Part of healthy living is learning to live with
moderation. In this passage, moderation allows
you to see God's plan more clearly. Consider an
excess in your life as you journey today. Is this
excess separating you from God?

*Loving God, we have created some obstacles
that obstruct our view of you. Give us the
strength to overcome these self-made barriers.*

Amen.

November 13

I have heard of your faith in the Lord Jesus and your love toward all the saints, and for this reason I do not cease to give thanks for you as I remember you in my prayers.

EPHESIANS 1:15–16

The Apostle Paul reminds us in this passage that in addition to giving thanks to God, we need to give thanks for each other. Take a moment today to remember those special people in your life whether they be family, friends, coworkers or maybe even strangers in whom you see God's presence.

Loving God, thank you for letting us see your light shining through people around us each day.

Amen.

November 14

These are the last words of David ... The God of Israel has spoken, the Rock of Israel has said to me: One who rules over people justly, ruling in the fear of God, is like the light of morning, like the sun rising on a cloudless morning, gleaming from the rain on the grassy land.

2 SAMUEL 23:1, 3—4

Refreshing leadership—that is the phrase that came to mind after reading these verses. Leadership which is both just and God-centered is like a perfect morning when you can sense the presence of God surrounding you.

Loving God, whether we lead a family or a work team, help us be the people you want us to be.

Amen.

November 15

*Then Pilate entered the headquarters again, summoned
Jesus, and asked him, "Are you King of the Jews?"
Jesus answered, "Do you ask this on your own, or did
others tell you about me?" Pilate replied, "I am not a
Jew, am I? Your own nation and the chief priests have
handed you over to me. What have you done?"*

JOHN 18:33–35

How influenced are you by the expressed
opinions of others? How often are your
opinions formed by what you have heard rather
than what you know? This passage reminds us how
damaging our comments about one another can be.

*Loving God, help us be discerning people
who are slow to judge each other.*

Amen.

November 16

*Then he will answer them, 'Truly I tell you,
just as you did not do it to one of the least of
these, you did not do it to me.'*

MATTHEW 25:45

Very often we talk about sin in language that
emphasizes our negative actions toward each
other. This passage reminds us of our sins of omission.

*Understanding God, you are steadfast in your
love of us. Give us strength to be more
steadfast in our care of each other.*

Amen.

November 17

"Therefore do not worry, saying, 'What will we eat?' or 'What will we drink?' or 'What will we wear?' ... But strive first for the kingdom of God and his righteousness, and all these things will be given to you as well."

MATTHEW 6:31, 33

Synonyms for strive include: struggle, try hard, attempt, do your best. In other words, striving first for the kingdom of God will not be easy, and you will not always hit the mark. Striving for the kingdom of God is a lifelong journey.

Loving God, as we journey toward a closer relationship with you, forgive all those times we fall short.

Amen.

November 18

*"O house of Jacob, come, let us walk
in the light of the Lord!"*
ISAIAH 2:5

Our neighborhoods are filled with hunger, sickness and violence. Against this backdrop, Isaiah offers us a glimpse of God's kingdom where weapons are turned into farm implements, where nations no longer engage in war. We have been challenged to live as active peacemakers.

*Gracious God, entrust us to your service as we
seek to walk in your light at all times.*

Amen.

November 19

*They shall build houses and inhabit them; they shall
plant vineyards and eat their fruit. They shall not
build and another inhabit; they shall not plant and
another eat; for like the days of a tree shall the days
of my people be, and my chosen shall long enjoy
the work of their hands.*

ISAIAH 65:21–22

When a tree loses a branch, the tree slowly
extends itself over the resulting wound,
sometimes leaving a knot or a scar. Other times, the
tree sends off shoots of new life around the broken
place, sometimes creating several new branches.
Either way, the tree is forever changed.

*Healer God, help us remain in communion
with you through life's trials so that we can
continue to grow despite the injuries incurred.*

Amen.

November 20

*Therefore encourage one another and build up
each other, as indeed you are doing.*
1 THESSALONIANS 5:11

God is our dwelling place. We are all in this
place together. My faith walk crisscrosses with
your faith walk. We should support, not hinder,
one another.

*Loving God, though we may sing
from different hymnals and read different
writings, you are the One all of us seek.
Help us to help each other.*

Amen.

November 21

See, I am sending my messenger to prepare the way before me, and the Lord whom you seek will suddenly come into his temple. The messenger of the covenant in whom you delight—indeed, he is coming, says the Lord of hosts.

Malachi 3:1

Journeys often have a purpose, getting from point A to point B being the most obvious. The Scripture challenges you to consider another reason for making a journey, and that is to deliver a message. Today, consider your role as a messenger for God.

Almighty God, walk with us this week as we consider the words and actions which communicate the message we are sending about your kingdom.

Amen.

November 22

Make me know your ways, O LORD;
teach me your paths.
PSALM 25:4

Ilike to think of our faith journey as an ongoing conversation with God. The purpose of our conversation is to help draw us closer to God's plan for us.

God of wonder, you can make the faith of a
mustard seed do amazing things. Continue
walking beside us as we continue in our
journey toward you.

Amen.

November 23

I will rejoice in Jerusalem, and delight in my people;
no more shall the sound of weeping be heard in it, or
the cry of distress. No more shall there be in it an
infant that lives but a few days, or an old person who
does not live out a lifetime; for one who dies at a
hundred will be considered a youth, and one who falls
short of a hundred will be considered accursed.

ISAIAH 65:19–20

It is not difficult to hear the weeping in our streets today—arguments, gunshots, ambulances and police sirens, to name a few. Consider today how you are a peacemaker amidst the chaos that surrounds us each day.

Lord God, illumine our hearts and make
us instruments of your peace.

Amen.

November 24

Come, behold the works of the LORD; see what
desolations he has brought on the earth. He makes
wars cease to the end of the earth; he breaks the bow,
and shatters the spear; he burns the shields with fire.

PSALM 46:8–9

Behold the works of the Lord: all wars will end and all the implements of war will be destroyed allowing for a lasting peace. Come Lord, come.

Gracious God, help us bring peace to our
neighborhoods and our cities so that we can
help bring peace to this world.

Amen.

November 25

Let me hear what God the LORD will speak, for he
will speak peace to his people, to his faithful, to
those who turn to him in their hearts. Surely his
salvation is at hand for those who fear him, that
his glory may dwell in our land.

PSALM 85:8–9

L ord, come and bring peace to all your people.
And until that day, let us visualize peace and
live into that vision as if it were reality.

Loving God, today we pray for the lasting
peace that only you can bring.

Amen.

November 26

As I watched in the night visions, I saw one like a human being coming with the clouds of heaven. And he came to the Ancient One and was presented before him. To him was given dominion and glory and kingship, that all peoples, nations, and languages should serve him. His dominion is an everlasting dominion that shall not pass away, and his kingship is one that shall never be destroyed.

DANIEL 7:13–14

I believe people who have joy and hope in their lives are better able to imagine a future in which they live in the abundance that God's kingdom offers. As people of faith, we are called to help others dream their dreams and feel empowered to live into them.

Loving God, help us help your children today. Let them see your active presence in their lives.

Amen.

November 27

*Restore us O Lord God of hosts; let your
face shine, that we may be saved.*
PSALM 80:19

Advent is a time of restoration—of ourselves
and of God's creation. Each of us has a vision
of God's kingdom. We should try to order our lives
and our actions in ways which live into that vision.

*Loving God, make us instruments of
restoration. Make us peacemakers. Make us
good stewards of the gifts you have given us.*

Amen.

November 28

In those days and at that time I will cause a righteous Branch to spring up for David; and he shall execute justice and righteousness in the land.

JEREMIAH 33:15

Advent is the time when Christians anticipate God dwelling among us through Jesus. It is a time of birth and rebirth. We are moving toward a new vision of the world, toward a renewed vision of God and toward a new vision of ourselves living in concert with God's plan for us.

Almighty God, be with us today as we begin our Advent journey. Help us move closer to you and your plan for us.

Amen.

November 29

"But about that day and hour no one knows, neither the angels of heaven, nor the Son, but only the Father ... Therefore you also must be ready, for the Son of Man is coming at an unexpected hour."

MATTHEW 24:36, 44

During the Advent season, we are asked to meditate on the Second Coming. We must always be ready to act in ways that build up God's kingdom.

Merciful God, bless us to your service. May our actions build up your kingdom. Forgive us when we do otherwise, and gently nudge us back toward your will.

Amen.

November 30

Take away from me the noise of your songs; I will not listen to the melody of your harps. But let justice roll down like waters, and righteousness like an ever-flowing stream.

AMOS 5:23–24

Worship and praise obviously have a place in our ongoing relationship with God, but this passage reminds us that our faith should make us different. Our faith should cause us to be seekers and doers of justice.

God of Justice, help us act in ways that are pleasing to you and helpful to the larger community of our brothers and sisters.

Amen.

December

In 1987, the Church Health Center first opened its doors in this historic home.

December 1

*And this is my prayer, that your love may overflow
more and more with knowledge and full insight to help
you to determine what is best, so that in the day of
Christ you may be pure and blameless, having
produced the harvest of righteousness that comes
through Jesus Christ for the glory and praise of God.*

PHILIPPIANS 1:9–11

Imagine the physical labor required to harvest a
field or vineyard in biblical times. With fewer
opportunities for movement in today's world, you
must be intentional about incorporating exercise
into your routine. Add steps to your day today. Walk
to a coworker's desk rather then sending another
email, or park in a space further from the entrance.

*God of the harvest, allow us
opportunities to sow seeds of justice,
honesty, virtue, and decency.*

Amen.

December 2

*John the Baptist went into all the regions around the
Jordan, proclaiming a baptism of repentance for the
forgiveness of sins, as it is written in the book of the
words of the prophet Isaiah, "The voice of one crying
out in the wilderness: 'Prepare the way of the Lord,
make his paths straight.'"*

LUKE 3:3–4

If time and weather permit, consider changing the
location of your walk today. Walk a new path and
imagine you are John the Baptist walking in the
wilderness. How does your life proclaim, "Prepare
the way of the Lord?" Consider praying for your
neighborhood as you walk today.

*Gracious God, thank you for giving
strength to our voices so that we can
better proclaim your truth.*

Amen.

December 3

The LORD has taken away the judgments
against you, he has turned away your enemies.
The king of Israel, the LORD, is in your midst;
you shall fear disaster no more.

ZEPHANIAH 3:15

As you walk today, walk with an attitude of
confidence even if you lack it yourself. God
wants you to live with confidence in yourself and
in the promises God has made for you. Pray today
for God to remove unneeded anxiety from your life.

Almighty God, help us remember that you
are always shouldering burdens with us,
so that we are never alone.

Amen.

December 4

Let your gentleness be known to
everyone. The Lord is near.

PHILIPPIANS 4:5

Is your gentleness like a light hidden under a basket? Do not hide the concern, the care, you have for others. Walk through each day as though the Lord is near, and be willing to make yourself vulnerable to others.

God of peace, as we walk among your children
today, may they see your face in ours.

Amen.

December 5

*May the God of steadfastness and encouragement
grant you to live in harmony with one another,
in accordance with Christ Jesus, so that together you
may with one voice glorify the God and Father of
our Lord Jesus Christ.*

ROMANS 15:5—6

At first glance, a barbershop quartet has little to do with our faith journey, but I couldn't help thinking about the seamless way four voices can blend to create amazing music. Each of us sings a different part, but today I ask you to consider the wonderful sound we can create if we "sing" in harmony with one another.

*Loving God, help us mold our own voices
then blend them with our neighbors' voices
into an amazing life-song.*

Amen.

December 6

May the God of hope fill you with all joy and
peace in believing, so that you may abound in hope
by the power of the Holy Spirit.

ROMANS 15:13

As children of God, we are challenged to see God in each of our neighbors, and in so doing we blend our voices into a beautiful harmony which is God's holy choir.

Gracious God, during this wonderful season,
fill us with the joy and peace that comes from
believing so that we may abound in hope.

Amen.

December 7

*The LORD opens the eyes of the blind. The LORD lifts
up those who are bowed down; the LORD loves the
righteous. The LORD watches over strangers; he
upholds the orphan and the widow.*

PSALM 146:8–9

Not all of us are eye care professionals, but all
of us are asked to help people see their lives
through new lenses. Not all of us are physicians or
physical therapists, but all of us are asked to help
people walk with their heads held higher. Being
such presences in people's lives is easier if we know
them, but we are asked to do the same to the
strangers among us.

*Healer God, help us bring sight to the blind
and strength to the lame. Help us to be more
welcoming to those strangers among us.*

Amen.

December 8

Be patient, therefore, beloved, until the coming
of the Lord. The farmer waits for the precious
crop from the earth, being patient with it until it
receives the early and the late rains. You must
also be patient. Strengthen your hearts, for the
coming of the Lord is near.

JAMES 5:7–8

As children of God, we have an obligation to care for one another. This requires us to be nurturing presences to those around us even if our efforts aren't met with smiling, happy faces.

Gentle God, thank you for all the people
who surround us. Give us the strength to
treat our neighbors as though we have
already walked a mile in their shoes.

Amen.

December 9

There was a man sent from God, whose name was John. He came as a witness to testify to the light, so that all might believe through him. He himself was not the light, but he came to testify to the light.

JOHN 1:6–8

Jesus said that we are the light of the world and that we should live our lives in a way that provides a beacon to God for others. Throughout this day, consider how your life shines light so that others may see.

Understanding God, you ask us to be living examples of our faith in you. For all those times we fall short of the mark, we thank you for your grace and forgiveness.

Amen.

December 10

Do not worry about anything, but in everything by prayer and supplication with thanksgiving let your requests be made known to God. And the peace of God, which surpasses all understanding, will guard your hearts and your minds in Christ Jesus.

PHILIPPIANS 4:6–7

The season of Advent is a short journey within the larger context of your life. But travel is almost always more fulfilling when you are joined by someone else. This passage notes that your life should be an ongoing conversation with God, that you are never alone on your journey.

God of our past, present and future, incline our ears to you so that we will be able to hear your still small voice guiding us.

Amen.

December 11

And he shall stand and feed his flock in the strength of the LORD, in the majesty of the name of the LORD his God. And they shall live secure, for now he shall be great to the ends of the earth; and he shall be the one of peace.

MICAH 5:4–5

God incarnate will be here soon. Be fervent in your prayers, gentle with one another and know that God, your Creator, remains steadfast by your side today and always.

Gracious, loving God, you have always been with us, but we are often blind to your presence. Guide us where you want us to go. Help us to move closer to you and your plan for us.

Amen.

December 12

And the crowds asked John the Baptist, "What then should we do?" In reply he said to them, "Whoever has two coats must share with anyone who has none; and whoever has food must do likewise."

LUKE 3:10–11

We are approaching a season of gift giving. Consider taking this passage literally. Take a few moments to survey your closet and find five items in good condition that might be useful to someone else. You could also go to the store and purchase some new items that might be helpful this time of the year. If you do not know a family in need, share these items with a local church, clothes closet or food pantry.

Merciful God, in this season of giving, help us be mindful of the needs of our brothers and sisters.

Amen.

December 13

*But you, O Bethlehem of Ephrathah, who are
one of the little clans of Judah, from you shall
come forth for me one who is to rule in Israel,
whose origin is from of old, from ancient days.*

MICAH 5:2

It is easy to feel insignificant in this world. We are preparing to celebrate a young girl in a small town giving birth to a little boy in whom the hope of the world will come to rest. God can do extraordinary things through unlikely people— including you.

*Almighty God, mold us and use us as
instruments of your will.*

Amen.

December 14

Restore us, O Lord God of hosts;
let your face shine, that we may be saved.

PSALM 80:19

"Restore our relationship with you, O God," cries the psalmist. Throughout the earthly ministry of Jesus, as he healed people, he also restored their relationship to their family, to their community and to God. Healing was a critical element to Christ's ministry, and it should be a primary element of our ministry to one another.

Healing God, be with us in our
ministry of restoration. Help us give
hope to all who come to us.

Amen.

December 15

Paul, a servant of Jesus Christ, called to be an apostle,
set apart for the gospel of God, which he promised
beforehand through his prophets in the holy scriptures,
the gospel concerning his Son, who was descended
from David according to the flesh.

ROMANS 1:1–3

I have often thought about my calling and whether I was living into the life God intended. This passage helped with a new perspective. Consider today how you are set apart rather than how you are called. What distinguishes you from others? What perspective do you bring to a table? Maybe it is in these answers that you will find your calling.

Loving God, help us discern those unique
ways you have molded us so that we might
more clearly see our calling.

Amen.

December 16

In the sixth month the angel Gabriel was sent by God to a town in Galilee called Nazareth to a virgin engaged to a man whose name was Joseph, of the house of David. The virgin's name was Mary. And he came to her and said, "Greetings, favored one! The Lord is with you."

LUKE 1:26–28

I t would be incredible for God to communicate with each of us as clearly as in this passage. I would guess, however, that most of you are like me. You have what is often a vague sense of what you think is God's will for you. It then becomes an important part of your faith journey how you live into that calling.

Merciful God, thank you for being with us this and every day. Continue to guide us as we try to do your will.

Amen.

December 17

Mary said to the angel, "How can this be since I am a
virgin?" The angel said to her, "The Holy Spirit will
come upon you, and the power of the Most High will
overshadow you; therefore the child to be born will be
holy; he will be called Son of God. And now, your
relative Elizabeth in her old age has also conceived a
son; for this is the sixth month for her who was said to
be barren. For nothing will be impossible with God."
LUKE 1:34–37

"For nothing will be impossible with God."
That short sentence sums up the message of
this season for me. During Advent of each year, we
are challenged to visualize a world where "the wolf
shall live with the lamb" and to recommit ourselves
to walk faithfully into that vision.

Almighty God, nothing is impossible with
you. Work through us in amazing ways so
that we can live in your peaceable kingdom.

Amen.

December 18

"My soul magnifies the Lord, and my spirit rejoices in God my Savior, for he has looked with favor on the lowliness of his servant. Surely, from now on all generations will call me blessed; for the Mighty One has done great things for me, and holy is his name."

LUKE 1:46–49

As part of your meditative time today, consider gifts you have received from God, maybe even writing them down. Throughout the day, consider this list, and thank God for all these gifts.

Generous God, thank you for the many blessings you have poured out on us. May we remain forever grateful of your generosity.

Amen.

December 19

Let the word of Christ dwell in you richly; teach and admonish one another in all wisdom; and with gratitude in your hearts sing psalms, hymns, and spiritual songs to God.

COLOSSIANS 3:16

I love the familiar hymns of Christmas. I tend to know them better, sing them louder, and smile while singing them. My prayer for each of you is that through this season of miracles, you have experienced Christ dwelling in you richly.

Gracious God, help us sense your presence so that the life-song we sing is authored by you.

Amen.

December 20

Now therefore, O kings, be wise; be warned, O rulers of the earth. Serve the LORD with fear, with trembling kiss his feet, or he will be angry, and you will perish in the way; for his wrath is quickly kindled. Happy are those who take refuge in him.

PSALM 2:10–12

Our world is in such turmoil. There is so much healing needed. Our passage today reminds us that our God is also the God of our leaders. Pray today for our leaders to hear God's will.

Almighty God, help our leaders hear your voice in their lives so that they might lead as you would have them.

Amen.

December 21

I will recount the gracious deeds of the LORD, the praiseworthy acts of the LORD, because of all that the LORD has done for us, and the great favor to the house of Israel that he has shown them according to his mercy, according to the abundance of his steadfast love.

ISAIAH 63:7

As we approach the end of the calendar year, we approach the season of inventory — businesses take inventory to see what remains on their shelves, many of us take personal inventory to see how we might enter the new year on a different and better note. We are reminded today that we should take inventory of all God has done for us.

Almighty God, thank you for your steadfast presence in our lives. Continue to mold us into the people you want us to be.

Amen.

December 22

Bear with one another and, if anyone has a complaint
against another, forgive each other; just as the Lord
has forgiven you, so you also must forgive. Above all,
clothe yourselves with love, which binds everything
together in perfect harmony.

COLOSSIANS 3:13–14

So much of the language of faith references how
people are to live in community. For those times
when living in community is difficult, we are
reminded by today's passage that forgiveness
should rule.

Almighty God, help us be more
forgiving people and help us be people
who are easy to forgive.

Amen.

December 23

I will greatly rejoice in the LORD, my whole being shall exult in my God; for he has clothed me with the garments of salvation, he has covered me with the robe of righteousness, as a bridegroom decks himself with a garland, and as a bride adorns herself with her jewels.

ISAIAH 61:10

I love the image of being clothed by God. It suggests an intimacy to the relationship I often overlook. Ours is not a God "over there" absent from us but a God uniquely and miraculously connected to us.

God of deliverance, God of justice, you have clothed us with your best. Help us live into the people you want us to be.

Amen.

December 24

*In the beginning was the Word, and the Word was
with God, and the Word was God.*

<small>JOHN 1:1</small>

"God So Loved the World" is an anthem often
sung at Easter, but I couldn't help singing
that one phrase over and over again this morning.
God became human, became flesh, and lived among
us. That is the gift of Christmas.

*Everlasting God, you understand us better
than we understand ourselves. Help us to
see ourselves and each other as if we are
looking through your eyes.*

Amen.

December 25

*Joseph went to be registered with Mary, to whom
he was engaged and who was expecting a child.
While they were there, the time came for her to
deliver her child. And she gave birth to her
firstborn son and wrapped him in bands of cloth,
and laid him in a manger, because there was no
place for them in the inn.*

LUKE 2:5–7

The image of Jesus' humble beginnings is
powerful. Consider the immigrants among you
today. Consider the children being born today in
modern day mangers far away from home. Pray for
them all.

*Almighty God, much of the hope of this
world rests in bundles of innocence being
born at this time. Help us to create a world
that is safer, more nurturing and more
loving for each of them.*

Amen.

December 26

And the Word became flesh and lived among us,
and we have seen his glory, the glory as of a
father's only son, full of grace and truth.

JOHN 1:14

God became one of us through Jesus. No one
understands the joy, the pain and the
complexities of our individual lives more than God.

Gracious God, help us accept that you know
and understand our every need.

Amen.

December 27

*In that region there were shepherds living in
the fields, keeping watch over their flock by
night. Then an angel of the Lord stood before
them, and the glory of the Lord shone around
them, and they were terrified.*

LUKE 2:8–9

I am moved by God's love of ordinary people. God
chose shepherds to be the first to hear of the birth
of the Messiah, and Jesus himself becomes known
as a shepherd of people.

*Gracious God, we are ordinary people. Help us
do extraordinary things in your name.*

Amen.

December 28

When the time had come for their purification
according to the law of Moses, they brought him up to
Jerusalem to present him to the Lord (as it is written in
the law of the Lord, "Every firstborn male shall be
designated as holy to the Lord"), as they offered a
sacrifice according to what is stated in the law of the
Lord, "a pair of turtledoves or two young pigeons."

LUKE 2:22–24

Throughout Leviticus, if one could not afford a
lamb or other expensive animal for a burnt-
offering, one was allowed to substitute "a pair of
turtledoves or two young pigeons." Today's
passage reflects yet another example of Jesus'
humble beginnings.

Almighty God, you could have chosen a royal
family for your son, but you chose a young
girl and a carpenter. Help us see your
handiwork in each person we meet today.

Amen.

December 29

*See, I am going to bring them from the land of the
north, and gather them from the farthest parts of
the earth, among them the blind and the lame,
those with child and those in labor, together; a
great company, then shall return here.*

JEREMIAH 31:8

God is promising to bring the people of Israel
and Judah back to the land that he gave to their
ancestors. God promises not only the able bodied,
but also those who might be considered a burden
to the others—the sick, the pregnant, the mothers
with young children.

*Loving God, following your example,
help us better care for all of your people
today and every day.*

Amen.

December 30

Praise the LORD, O Jerusalem! Praise your God, O Zion! For he strengthens the bars of your gates; he blesses your children within you.

PSALM 147:12–13

"Praise God for everything he has done for you!" implores the psalmist. As we approach the end of the year, take a moment to praise God for the blessings which have been bestowed upon you this year.

Almighty God, for your steadfast presence in our lives this year, we give you thanks.

Amen.

December 31

*He grants peace within your borders; he fills
you with the finest of wheat.*

PSALM 147:14

I appreciate that peace and sustenance are side-by-side in this verse. On a fundamental level, people want to be able to take care of themselves, their families, and their loved ones. If this is seen as impossible, then violent acts might become a considered option. Programs that reach out to those less fortunate—health ministries, food pantries and clothes closets—help make the world a safe, more peaceful place for all God's children.

*Loving God, help each of us as we seek to
be peacemakers in our own ways. May our
efforts on your behalf bring hope and
healing to our neighbors.*

Amen.

*As God's chosen ones, holy and beloved,
clothe yourselves with compassion,
kindness, humility, meekness and patience.*
COLOSSIANS 3:12

*Loving God, help us be the people
you want us to be.*

Amen.

Notes

Notes

William L. "Butch" Odom, Jr. is Director of Faith Community Outreach at the Church Health Center in Memphis, Tennessee. He began his career at the Church Health Center in 1991 as the business manager. As the Church Health Center has expanded, Butch has served in a variety of roles. He is the author of *Walking to the Cross: A Devotional for Lent* and several pieces for *Church Health Reader*, including the award-winning reflection, "Setting a New Table." Butch and his wife Debbie live in Memphis where they are members of First Congregational Church.